BOLD TO SAY

Learning and Living the Lord's Prayer

Dr. Geoffrey Lentz

New Fire Press
Pensacola, Florida
2025

Copyright © 2025, Geoffrey D. Lentz.
All Rights Reserved.

Unless otherwise marked, scripture quotations are taken from the New Revised Standard Version Updated Edition . Copyright © 2021 National Council of Churches of Christ in the United States of America. Used by permission. All rights reserved worldwide.

Cover Design: Jeb Eugene Hunt

ISBN: 978-1-63199-939-0
eISBN: 978-1-63199-940-6

New Fire Press
6 East Wright Street
Pensacola, FL 32501

newfirepress.com

Dedication

To Pensacola First United Methodist Church—
a people shaped by prayer,
bold enough to say
and courageous enough to live.

And to all who seek the courage
to pray with lips and lives,
may you discover here
the boldness of words
that shape the kingdom
and reshape us all.

Acknowledgements

Special thanks to my wife, Liz—whose patience, encouragement, and grace make every project possible—and to the good people of First United Methodist Church of Pensacola, whose faithfulness inspires me daily.

My gratitude goes to my brother, Jeb Hunt—partner in many projects—whose creativity shaped this book through his beautiful cover design and thoughtful layout.

I am also deeply grateful to Kari Barlow for her keen editorial insight, and to Henry Neufeld for his publishing wisdom. Thanks to the Rev. Emily Kincaid, my co-worker and friend, and to Sharolyn and Tom Hunt, my mother and stepfather, whose encouragement and enthusiasm gave me the boldness to see this project through to publication.

Above all, thanks be to God, from whom all blessings flow.

Table of Contents

	Dedication	iii
	Acknowledgements	iv
1	Our Father, who art in heaven, hallowed be thy name	1
2	Thy kingdom come, thy will be done on earth as it is in heaven	17
3	Give us this day our daily bread	31
4	Forgive us our trespasses as we forgive those who trespass against us	45
5	Lead us not into temptation but deliver us from evil	59
6	For Thine is the kingdom, the power, and the glory, forever	75
7	Amen	89
	Scripture Index	99

1

Our Father, who art in heaven, hallowed be thy name

The first thing that members of the early church taught a new convert was how to pray the Lord's Prayer. They did this because to learn this prayer is to be introduced to the entire Christian faith. This prayer touches every aspect of scripture and provides a framework for the Christian life. It's a faith and a life that does not come naturally to us; it must be taught. Disciples are made, not born. Jesus' disciples knew that they needed assistance, so they petitioned him, "Teach us to pray." The Lord's Prayer is his answer.

A Lot to Learn

If most of us are honest, we will admit that we do not always feel successful in our prayer life. In my ministry, I have encountered hundreds of people who feel as if their spirituality is inadequate. I have often been frustrated with my own prayer life. Despite my desire to be holy and my desire to be a person with a deep connection to God, it just doesn't seem to work. As a professional holy person, I have searched the world over to learn new prayer practices and strategies to aid my spiritual growth, but many days I still feel as though my prayer life is rudimentary at best.

A few years ago, I decided to go on a spiritual retreat with other Methodists from my area to a Benedictine monastery to learn about prayer. They ran out of rooms in the retreat center, so they put me up in a cell in the monastery proper with the monks. There on a table was a letter of welcome along with an invitation to pray the hours, share their meals, and enjoy community time in the pool hall (monks are fun too).

On my first morning, while it was still dark, I startled awake at the ringing of a bell right outside of my room at 5:45 in the morning. Squinting at my information sheet, I saw that the service of vigils was at 6:00 a.m. Not realizing that all the Methodist pilgrims were on a different schedule, I quickly got ready for morning prayer with the monks. The gothic chapel was shrouded in darkness, and only a few reading lights shone in the choir stalls. After finding a seat in the choir loft, I felt a little awkward and started to wonder if I was in the wrong place. The monks, dressed in black robes, filed into the chapel in complete silence. The background information on the monastery explained that these monks keep silence, except for prayer, until after breakfast. They all seemed either deep in prayer or half asleep—it was hard to tell.

Glancing around the chapel, I did not see any of the other members of my group. I was definitely in the wrong place. Wishing I had just stayed in bed, I reached to find the proper prayer manual and the proper corresponding Psalter. I was overwhelmed by the sheer number of prayer books from which to choose and decided to do what I always do when I am in over my head—fake it. Then, an older monk well into his 80s, with a wrinkled face and a long, white beard, approached me. In an act of hospitality, he broke his vow of silence for the day, asking, "Do you know how to use these?" I shook my head because I could not speak. He found the appropriate books, laid out each one, and pointed out the proper psalms with his fingers.

The monk returned to his stall as the service began, but after a prayer or two, he came back and explained that he had made a mistake and said to me, "Even after all these years, I am still learning to pray." We prayed the scripture, and we sang the Lord's Prayer together. That is the moment I realized that you can be an eighty-year-old monk in a monastery praying every day for most of your life and still have much to learn about prayer.

Christian prayer is not something that you master. It's something that you learn, humbly and respectfully over time. Christian prayer is not for spiritual masters but for disciples—disciples of Jesus.

ABCs of Faith

That is the powerful thing about the Lord's Prayer: it has the capacity to teach people at all points in their faith journey. It is the first prayer that we teach our children. When Luther wrote his *Shorter Catechism* to teach the basics of the Christian faith, he designed it with his own children in mind. He based the entire book on the Lord's Prayer. This prayer is the alphabet of Christianity. It gives us the vocabulary and grammar of our faith so we can begin to speak like Christians.

There is a story that preachers love to tell about a little girl who volunteered to lead a prayer in church. At the pulpit, she closed her eyes and began to recite the alphabet. When she finished, an older church member reprimanded her, asking, "What were you thinking? That was not a prayer." The girl, with childlike wisdom, replied, "I didn't know what words to use, so I thought I would just give God all the letters and let God spell whatever God wanted." When we pray the Lord's Prayer, we give God all the letters that are needed. When we don't know what to pray, this prayer is sufficient. It teaches us how to pray. But the Lord's Prayer is not solely for beginners. It is a prayer into which we never fully grow. In *The Lord and his Prayer*, leading New Testament scholar N.T Wright tells us:

> the prayer is not the spiritual version of the baby's mug and spoon set, though it is

that as well. It is the suit of clothes designed for us to wear in our full maturity. And most of us, putting the suit on week by week, have to realize that it's still a bit big for us, that we still have some growing to do before it'll fit.[1]

Wright goes on to say it's like going into our big brother's room and trying on his suit, knowing it is too big for us, but looking in mirror and impersonating our big brother, trying for just a moment to be our big brother. This prayer is too big for us, but it helps us know where we need to grow.

In this image, our big brother is Jesus. Our big brother taught us to pray to our Father. This prayer is his prayer. While the traditional title of the prayer is the Our Father, it's the protestant title, the Lord's Prayer, that helps us realize this was Jesus' prayer before it was ours. We pray it because he prayed it. We can say, "Our Father," because he prayed to his father. This prayer is centered in Jesus.[2]

"Our"

The first thing to notice about the prayer is that it is corporate. Some religions teach you to go off and pray by yourself, and there is room for that in Christianity, but even when a hermit hiding deep in a cave prays a Christian prayer, he is not alone.

---

1 N. T. Wright, *The Lord and His Prayer.* (Grand Rapids, MI: Wm. B. Eerdmans Publishing, 2014), 2.
2 See Chapter 1 Reflection Question 1 for further group or individual refection on n page 14.

Christians are never alone; we pray together. To say, "Our Father," is to admit that we need one another and that God does not belong to any one of us. To pray the Lord's Prayer is to acknowledge that we need the church.

Vincent Donovan tells a wonderful story about being a missionary to the Masai people in Africa. He had begun to teach the village about the basics of Christian faith in order to prepare the entire village for baptism. But Donovan had concerns about one man in the village and shared his reservations with Ndongoya, the village elder. "This old man sitting here has missed too many of our instruction meetings. He was always out herding cattle. He will not be baptized with the rest." Ndongoya stopped him, asking, "Padri, why are you trying to break us up and separate us? During this whole year that you have been teaching us, we have talked about these things when you were not here, at night around the fire. Yes, there have been lazy ones in this community, but they have been helped by those with much energy. There are stupid ones in the community, but they have been helped by those who are intelligent. There are ones with little faith in this village, but they have been helped by those with much faith. Would you turn out and drive off the lazy ones and the ones with little faith and the stupid ones? From the first day I have spoken for these people. And I speak for them now. Now, on this day one year later, I can declare for them and for all this community that we have reached the step in our lives where we can say, "We believe."[3]

Praying to "our" Father means that we are a part of a family. This concept is a helpful corrective to a modern world that focuses so heavily on the individual and his or her rights. The rabid individualism of the enlightenment often finds its way into church, but there is no place for it in God's family. When we cannot pray, our sisters and brothers pray for us. When we do not have the words, those gifted with words use them on our behalf. When we lack faith, our friends lend us theirs, much like the paralyzed man's friends did when they lowered him through the ceiling to Jesus. It was because of their faith that Jesus healed him (Luke 5:20). Our community—not only the church here on earth but all the company of heaven, the community of saints—carries us when we cannot manage on our own. When we pray, the saints are praying with us; the great cloud of witnesses cheer us on as we run our race (Hebrews 12). To pray as a Christian means to never pray alone. And the most exciting thing about this blessed community called church is that the primary member is Jesus, our older brother. To say, "Our Father," is to be a part of Jesus' family, to call his father ours, and know that when we pray, he prays with us and for us (Hebrews 7:25, Romans 8:34, 1 John 2:1).[4]

---

3   Vincent Donovan, Quoted in *Liturgy*, Edited by Gabe Huck, (Chicago: Liturgy Training Publications, 1994), 18-19.
4   See Reflection Question 2 on page 14.

"Father"

The second word of the prayer, "Father," is the most important word of the entire prayer. Today the word *father* is a stumbling block to many. To some, it implies that God has a human gender. The masculinization of the deity has supported patriarchy and other forms of oppression. Others, having a poor relationship with their own father find this image of God unhelpful. My mentor, Wesley Wachob, teaches, "God is nothing like your father. God is God. Your father, every now and then, by the grace and mercy of God, might be a bit like God." This analogy only works one way. The use of *father* here is not meant to give identity to God, but to give identity to us who pray it. We are God's children now. The title of father does not mean that God is male. God is a spirit who is beyond human gender. The book of Genesis teaches that we are created in God's image both "male and female."[5]

Father, as used in the Lord's Prayer, signifies not gender but relationship. In their book, *Lord, Teach Us: The Lord's Prayer & the Christian Life*, William Willimon and Stanley Hauerwas help us see this clearly:

---

[5] Many of our mainline denominations, including my own, have well intentioned statements that say that God is non-gendered, but I think that it is more theologically faithful to say that God is gendered. However, God's gender which includes both male and feminine attributes (and who knows what else) is best described as God. Or, as my friend, Rev. Brennan Peacock, says, "God's gender is God."

In calling God Father we are speaking first and foremost about Jesus' relationship to God, not our own. That is to say, God is called Father because we have come to know Jesus as the Son. "Father" and "Son" is the way that we have been taught to name a certain relationship within the inner life of God. The important thing is not that these two terms are of the male gender, for Christians have always believed that God is greater than any human conceptions of gender. What is important is that these names attempt to describe the familial relationship that is part of God's own life. We can't say "Father" without remembering the Son; we can never know the Father unless the Son reveals the Father to us.[6]

We can claim God as our father only because of what Jesus has done for us. Jesus is the Son of God, who came and brought us salvation so we could also be God's sons and daughters. Paul says that Christ gives us the spirit of adoption (Romans 8). Through Christ, we are made part of God's family. It is because Jesus is God's Son that we can now, through him, call God our Father.[7]

---

6   William Willimon and Stanley Hauerwas, *Lord Teach Us to Pray*, (Nashville, TN: Abingdon Press, 1996), 29-30.
7   See Refection Question 3 on page 14

Relationship

In other words, the power of Christian prayer is not found in a host of cool techniques. If you are looking for those kinds of spiritual exercises, you might try a different religion. If you are looking for magic words, other traditions have incantations. The Christian faith is not focused on spells or charms or deep meditation practices. The power of Christian prayer—what makes it work—is our relationship with God. This is the core of gospel.

I used to be bothered that our Eastern friends had so many wonderful techniques to accompany their religions and philosophies. The time-honored practices of meditation and yoga are fascinating and certainly have amazing health benefits, but they're not what Christian prayer is about. In the Christian faith, prayer is not a technique for us to get something out of God. It is a technique for God to get something out of us. Our relationship with God does not exist because of anything we do or say. It exists solely because of the grace God extends to us.

In Douglas Adams' hilarious sci-fi story, *The Hitchhiker's Guide to the Galaxy*, a futuristic society develops a super computer tasked with discovering the ultimate answer "to Life the Universe and Everything." But just before it was finished computing the last bit of information, it was destroyed. A group of philosophers and psychologists teamed up to put an end to the project because they were worried about losing their jobs. One of the philosophers asks, "What's the use of our sitting up half the night arguing that there may or may not be a God if this machine only goes and gives you his bleeding phone number the next morning?" That is what the Lord's Prayer does. In this prayer, Jesus gives us a direct line of communication to God. That direct line is Jesus. Jesus makes our human methods of reaching God obsolete. Techniques, strategies, and formulas do not work. What works is God coming to us. God is with us, and because of that, we can pray.

God in Jesus Christ has come to you—he prays with you and for you and has put you in a relationship with his father, the Lord Almighty. Christian prayer is not a technique but a relationship. This relationship changes everything. In the traditional Anglican liturgy, the call to prayer for the Lord's Prayer begins with, "Now as our Savior Christ hath taught us, we are bold to say..." Growing up hearing this call to prayer, I always wondered why we need such boldness. Yet, it is boldness that is required.

We must recover the idea of how strange a thing it is to pray. We are lifting up our poor words, ignorant phrases, even minor requests to the one "Who art in heaven." This phrase means that God is the one who created the cosmos, who sits outside of space and time. The fact that God's dwelling place is in heaven reminds us that God is the Lord, the Almighty, the King of Creation, the one who is a consuming fire, and before whom the earth shakes.

"Hallowed"

Furthermore, God is a holy God. When we pray, "Hallowed be thy name," we are affirming God's holiness. This word, holy, is often misunderstood. It is not about being a goody-goody and following all the rules just right. Instead the word holy means to be set apart, different, or unusual. I have come to believe that the best way to define holy is to drill down to the original sense of the word, which is *weird*. The Old English word *weird* was a religious term. It meant something that was supernatural or other worldly. To be weird is to be different from the status quo of our world. Describing God as holy is saying that God is weird, unlike anything we have ever known. In fact, this God is unknowable by human beings. The only way to know such a weird God is by God revealing Godself to us.

Several years ago, officials in Austin, Texas, decided to create a marketing campaign for the city. Instead of trying to copy Los Angeles, New York City, Chicago, or Washington, D.C., they chose to be themselves—weird. They came up with the slogan, "Keep Austin weird." It became an incredibly successful promotion that captured the unique nature of that Texas community. As Christians, we must keep God weird. The God we worship does not think as we do. This God will not be our pet or mascot—only our Lord. To worship a weird God whose name is hallowed is to become weird. As the scriptures say, "You shall be holy as I am holy" (Leviticus 20:26, 1 Peter 1:16). Or put another way: You shall be weird—as I am weird. The church, because it worships a holy God, ought to be different from the world, embodying faith, hope, and love in the midst of darkness.[8]

The Lord's Prayer begins with the notion that God is in heaven and that God is holy, emphasizing the transcendent nature of God. Danish philosopher, poet, and theologian Soren Kierkegaard taught us that there is "an infinite categorical distinction" between us and God. God is the creator and we are creatures. As the old man outside a gas station told me when I asked for directions to a country church, "You can't get there from here." There is no resource or ability within the grasp of humanity to reach God. God is in heaven, and we are on earth. God is holy, and human beings are not.

Boldness

If we had any sense at all, I think we would keep our mouths shut and refrain from prayer entirely. Surely this God would be too busy to care about my sick friend, my child's cold, or whether it has rained recently in my zip code. Surely this God would be too busy, too important, and too transcendent to care whether I pray or not. Praying to God, rightly understood, is a terrifying thing—or as Proverbs says over and over, "the fear of the Lord is the beginning of wisdom." Fear and awe is the beginning of wisdom, but it is not the end. The great wisdom of God is the cross of Christ that bridges the gap

---

8   See Reflection Question 4 on page 14.

between humanity and God. Jesus' prayer gives us this boldness (1 Corinthians 3).

Theologian Frederick Buechner, in *Whistling in the Dark: A Doubter's Dictionary*, says, "It is only the words 'Our Father' that make the whole thing bearable. If God is indeed something like a father, then as something like children maybe we can risk approaching him anyway."[9] The Lord's Prayer gives us the boldness to talk to God as though we are God's children, because through Jesus we are.

I read a newspaper article about a sixty-seven-year-old man named John Moore who lives in Tampa. An avid golfer, he had golfed every day for the past twenty years. A reporter asked him why he did it every day. He said, "Well, you can't play this game one, two days a week. You have to play it all the time if you want to do something with it." Prayer is like that—you have to keep at it. But then the article turned in a strange and surprising direction, explaining that John did not play on a real golf course. The only golf he played consisted of going into the middle of the median on Interstate 275 in downtown Tampa where he hits thirty-five long-iron shots. The reporter asked again why he did it, and John Moore said his dream was to one day "get good enough to play on an actual course." After twenty years of practice, he still was not ready for a real game of golf.[10]

---

9 Frederick Buechner, *Whistling in the Dark: A Doubter's Dictionary*. (San Francisco, CA: HarperSanFrancisco, 1988), 84.

10 News of the Weird Column, Read in the Pensacola Independent Paper circa 2009.

I think sometimes our prayer lives are like that. We play on the median instead of the course. We are afraid to pray because we want to have the right words and, like John Moore, we want to "get good enough." But none of that matters when it comes to Christian prayer. The important thing is not knowing exactly how to pray but knowing to whom you are praying. God is the Father of our Lord Jesus Christ, the one who raised him from the dead. That is why we can have the boldness to pray, "Our Father." As God's children, we can boldly go before his throne of grace (Romans 12). The Lord's Prayer bridges the gap between humanity and God without reducing God's holiness or power. Through Jesus, we can lift up our weak and trembling voices, our imperfect words, and broken techniques to join the mighty chorus of saints and angels. Despite our weakness and inadequacies, as God's children we can boldly say, "Our Father."[11]

Reflection Questions

1. Where are you in your spiritual journey and prayer life? Are you just beginning, have you taken a new turn, or have you been on the road for a while? In what ways has the Lord's Prayer meant different things to you along the way?
2. To pray this prayer means to be in community with others. How does the communal nature of the Our Father change the way we pray it?

---

11 See Reflection Question 5 on page 14.

3. How does understanding "Father" as a Christocentric term, one that can be understood only through Jesus, affect the nature of praying the prayer?
4. In what ways are disciples of Jesus called to be weird?
5. How does this prayer give you boldness to pray? How has it changed your relationship with God?

2

Thy kingdom come, thy will be done on earth as it is in heaven

The early church decided to center all prayer and worship on the Lord's Prayer. It was added to every worship service, no matter the season. In the culinary realm, a host of spices are known for making food more flavorful—cumin and cayenne for Mexican cuisine, curry and turmeric for Indian, parsley and garlic for Italian, and the list goes on. But salt and pepper are universal spices. Every recipe I know calls for these two ingredients. They go with everything. It's like this one pair of loafers in my closet. Unlike my dress shoes, sneakers, and flip-flops, they look great with everything. That's the way it is with the Lord's Prayer—it goes with anything, because in it everything is included.

The *Didache*, the oldest known Christian text outside of the Bible, tells Christians to pray the Our Father three times a day. Praying this prayer regularly is an important Christian practice. It's what Christians do—whether we're gathering publicly for worship or privately for devotion. To be a Christian is to pray the Lord's Prayer. But do we understand what we are praying when we speak its words?

Prayer Lists

After the prologue that addresses a holy God in heaven through Jesus, the prayer moves to the petitions. Petitions are those things we want God to do. Our prayers are full of petitions. We want God to help us and our loved ones with whatever problems we might be facing. We're even pretty organized about it—hence the ubiquitous *prayer list*, detailing all that we want God to do for us. Beseeching God with faithful, open hearts is a good thing, but sometimes I worry that these petitions for ourselves and those dear to us have become the core of the church's prayer life. There is room in Christian prayer for our petitions, but that type of prayer is really not very different from pagan prayers where spirituality is used to get what we want from the divine realm. When many Christian groups gather for prayer, the lists go on and on. These prayer request can seem like a competition for who has the most woes or who is the most compassionate. At their worst, they can feel like gossip sessions where we are informing people about the issues of others rather than bearing one another's burdens and commending these cares to God.

Contrary to popular thought, God is not a cosmic Santa Claus whose purpose is to give us what we want. The primary purpose of Christian prayer is not to list our troubles, grievances, and woes. It is not meant to be an exercise in theological narcissism. Instead, we are to pray as Christ has taught us. Such a prayer might include our desires, but it has a markedly different focus. In fact, within the Lord's Prayer, the only place we find the concept of intercession is in the petition for daily bread. The remainder of the entire prayer is focused on God.

The first and primary petition of the Lord's Prayer is peculiar, but it establishes the proper focus. The request is for God's kingdom to come and for God's will be done on earth as it is done in heaven. Instead of laying out all of our wants and needs, we begin by asking God to shape those wants and needs. To pray this petition for the kingdom is to be willing to have our desires transformed into God's desires.[12]

When I was in high school, my favorite Bible verse was Psalm 37:4, "Delight yourself in the Lord, and he will give you the desires of your heart." What I liked about this verse so much was that it seemed to say to me that if I focused on God and prayed hard, God would reward me by giving me what I wanted. My prayers sounded something like this: "God, I'll do good for you if you do good for me. Scratch my back, God, and I'll scratch yours." It would be a pretty good deal to have with the Almighty, a symbiotic relationship for our mutual advantage. But the Almighty is not a business partner or Bob Barker itching to make a deal. God is God. Too often this *quid pro quo* spirituality reigns in the church. It diminishes the sovereignty of God and the Lordship of Christ and elevates humanity to a place of equal footing with God.

---

12 See Chapter 2 Reflection Question 1

I remember talking with my youth director one day about this verse, and she said, "There is something strange that happens when you delight yourself in the Lord. Instead of the Lord simply giving you what you want, the Lord causes you to want different things." Then she added, "If you delight yourself in the Lord, the desires of your heart will be the Lord's desires. When you pray for what God wants, that is a prayer that Jesus will always answer." As a teenager, I felt like prayer was a trick, a catch-22. *If you pray like a Christian, Jesus will answer your prayers. The only trouble is, your prayers will no longer be your prayers—but God's prayer.* Jesus says it another way in Matthew 6, telling his disciples, "Seek first the kingdom of heaven and all else will be added unto you." Prayer is about conforming our desires to God's. Christians pray, not to get what we want out of God, but for God to get what God wants out of us. That is the core of Christian spirituality. Willimon and Hauerwas state, "Prayer in Jesus' name is lifelong training in taking God's will a little more seriously and our own will a little less."[13] The act of surrendering our will, even in small bits over time, is not only challenging, it's unnatural, yet there it stands as the fundamental lesson Jesus is teaching with his model prayer.

---

13 William H. Willimon and Stanley Hauerwas, *Lord, Teach Us: The Lord's Prayer and the Christian Life* (Nashville: Abingdon Press, 1996), 69.

God's List

Jesus tells us our heavenly Father knows what we need before we ask (Matthew 6:8). That is important because most of the time we do not know what we need. We do not even know what we want. Many of the traditional Anglican and Methodist prayers begin with, "Almighty Father, who knows our needs before we ask and our ignorance in asking." That place of trust is where Christian prayer begins. When we pray this way, we trust God enough to believe that it does not all come down to us. That we do not need to have all the answers, the proper techniques, or the right words. Just the assurance that God loves us and knows what we need better than we do.

To pray like a Christian is to trust God. Paul teaches us in Romans 8 that when we don't know how to pray, we invite the Holy Spirit to come and pray for us—with inward groans—or "sighs too deep for words." The point here is that Christian prayer reflects trust in a God who prays for us, knows what we need, and provides. In Luke 11, Jesus again focuses on our unique relationship that he has given us to where God is "our Father." He says that our earthly parents would not feed us snakes and scorpions when we ask for fish or eggs. God, Jesus teaches us, loves us even more than our parents and wants to give us even better things. Then Luke's Gospel adds one more line from Jesus that helps us understand prayer. He says: "How much more will your Father in heaven give the Holy Spirit to those who ask him!" The primary gift we should be praying for is the spirit of God. This is the gift that is cherished above all others.[14]

I once was taught that when we pray, our focus should be telling God exactly what we want. I read in a well-known book on spirituality that we should not end all our prayers with the phrase, "Your will be done." This line of thinking says this is a weak way of praying, a copout, and we should have the boldness to pray for what we want. Other traditions say that we must "name it and claim it." Tell God what we want and say that it is already ours. It is true that there is a place in Christian prayer to say whatever is on our hearts, but the goal of Christian prayer is for our desires to be changed. Praying for God's will to be done is not a copout or a weak prayer. No, to pray this way is to pray like Jesus. In fact, it seems to be the most powerful prayer we can pray. The Lord's Prayer does not just end with this petition; it begins with it.

There is no more powerful prayer than one asking God to do what God wants to do. We see Jesus model this type of prayer throughout his life. When his hour had come and his very life was required of him, Jesus went alone to the garden of Gethsemane, and there he prayed, "Father, if this cup could be taken from me, but not my will but yours be done." What a powerful example of the how he continually taught his disciples to pray. Jesus mention his desire to live, but he submits his will to his

---

14   See Chapter 2 Reflection Question 2.

father. To pray in this manner is to open ourselves up, vulnerable before God. It is to offer ourselves entirely to God. To pray this way is to stand at the foot of the cross.[15]

In the field of church growth, many consultants have techniques and tools for a church to perform. If a church just had this ministry or that type of music, things would be better. I'm not sure that works. I think that the only surefire way to move forward is to perform an analysis of the bottlenecks. God wants to bring the kingdom of heaven to your church. The Holy Spirit has gifts that need to be poured out and people who need to be reached like the early Christians at Pentecost.

The Lord has desires and plans for your church to grow and make more disciples, but there are places where that growth is stifled. And I have discovered that if you do not know where the bottlenecks are, you're likely part of the problem. I have learned this the hard way, too often being insensitive to where God was already working. It's my tendency to start a project and say, "God, come and help me accomplish my plan." The result? Frustration. Every single time. But when I have prayed, "God, where is your plan? I want to help and serve you," I have been overwhelmed with blessings. This is what the Lord's Prayer does; it gets us out of God's way and aligns our desires with God's. It clears our bottle-

---

[15] See Chapter 2 Reflection Question 3

necks and allows the blessings of the kingdom to pour in. [16]

Political Speech

To pray for God's "will to be done" is the same thing as praying for God's "kingdom to come." It is to ask God to be God. To pray for a kingdom is strange to our modern ears. We have states and governments but not too many kingdoms. A kingdom is a realm ruled by a sovereign—a king. In other words, to pray the Lord's Prayer is to fall headlong into politics.

This is political speech. We can get the idea, as Christians, that the kingdom of heaven is a spiritual, ethereal thing found out there in the heavens or maybe inside our hearts. But by using political terms, Jesus took the most sacred and holy idea of God's reign and mixed it up with the most mundane and earthly concern—politics. The politics we are used to are nasty. They are about power and money, winning and losing. To pray for God's kingdom to come is to invite God into our political world.

What do the politics of Jesus look like? They are unlike the partisan politics to which we are accustomed. Jesus sums up his political platform in the Beatitudes. Once when teaching a group of middle school students on this subject, I needed a kinesthetic hook to make the lesson a little more engaging. I had each of them stand on their heads as they read the Beatitudes. We took turns holding their

---

16 See Chapter 2 Reflection Question 4.

feet. At some point, they determined that it was my turn. It took several people to hold my legs up against the wall. The blood rushed to my head. I looked around and the world seemed so strange. When I read the Beatitudes this way, they finally made more sense. Jesus' view of the world was completely upside down. In his kingdom, the poor are blessed, the meek win, those who are hungry for justice find it, and the lowly are lifted up. These are the politics of the kingdom of God. Radically different from the politics of our self-interest, they herald transformation and restoration and a way of living that is shaped by love of neighbor.[17]

That strange goal of Christian prayer is what I have struggled with the most. When I want to be a deeply spiritual person focused solely on God, I find that God sends my love and devotion elsewhere. In my study, I have a picture of a monk in prayer—St. Simeon the Stylite, my patron saint—that keeps this principle in my mind. What I admire about him is that he wanted to live deep in Christian spirituality. He left the city and retreated to the deserts of Syria to pray, but people kept bothering him. To cut down on interruptions, he built a forty-foot tower with a platform on the top. Simeon climbed the tower to be alone with God and lived there for more than forty years, never coming down. Is that what Christian spirituality looks like? No! There is more to the story.

---

17   See Chapter 2 Reflection Question 5.

For Christians, loving God means also loving our neighbors. And that kind of love isn't aloof or cloistered behind physical or emotional walls. When you think about it, you see that Christian spirituality is not very spiritual at all. It is firmly anchored in the earthly realm, manifesting as a hands-on love for God's people. Something strange happened when Simeon climbed the tower to escape his neighbors and be closer to God. Soon people from all over the world came to ask him to preach. At times, more than thirty thousand people gathered to speak to him. What great irony—the closer we get to God, the closer we are to people. Simeon could not run away from people into the desert or up on a platform because he was running to God. You cannot love God and not love your neighbor.

We have heard the saying, "He is so heavenly minded, he is no earthly good." That is not Christian spirituality. But if we view the world through the lens of the Lord's Prayer, we see that the more heavenly minded you are, the more down to earth you are. Willimon and Hauerwas explain it this way:

Our goal is not to fill you with enough spiritual hot air that you float a foot above the earth. Our goal is to teach you to pray in such a way that material matters like politics and bread will be for you spiritual matters.[18]

That is the radical nature of the Kingdom of heaven. It is not for heaven out there. It is for God's will to be done here on earth as it is in heaven.

---

18 Willimon & Hauerwas, *Lord Teach Us*, 50.

Christianity is not about people being snatched up out of earth to heaven. Our goal is not primarily to go to heaven when we die but have heaven come here. That is the vision we find in the final chapter of Revelation—the New Jerusalem coming down out of heaven to earth. Uniting with creation was the creator's goal all along. It is our prayer that heaven and earth will one day be the same place. That is what we mean when we say *thy kingdom come*. It is a prayer that transforms our actions and shapes us into citizen of the kingdom of heaven.[19]

Revolution

We don't have a clue what we are truly asking God for when we pray the Lord's Prayer. We are asking for revolution. To pray these words is to be a revolutionary—a radical. To pray this prayer takes more boldness than we can imagine. In *Wishful Thinking: A Seeker's ABC*, Frederick Buechner sums it up this way:

> We are asking God to do not what we want but what God wants. We are asking God to make manifest the holiness that is now mostly hidden, to set free in all its terrible splendor the devastating power that is now mostly under restraint. "Thy kingdom come...on earth" is what we are saying. And if that were suddenly to happen, what then? What would stand and what would

---

19 See Chapter 2 Reflection Question 6.

fall? Who would be welcomed in, and who be thrown the hell out? ... Boldness indeed. To pray those words is to invite the tiger out of the cage, to unleash a power that makes atomic power look like a warm breeze.[20]

Praying for the kingdom to come is an act of resistance. To pray the Lord's Prayer is to ask for revolution not only out in the world but in your life. And in a way that will open you up to God. Too much of our prayer life is consumed with attempts to control the world, to control God, but true Christian prayer is about surrendering our will, our desire, and our lives to God. The goal of prayer is not to change God. God is unchangeable. The primary goal is not even to change the world. The goal is to change you.

There is no more difficult prayer to pray than "thy kingdom come, thy will be done." To pray this way is to join Jesus in Gethsemane and take up your cross and follow him to Golgotha. The scariest part of praying this prayer is that it is one prayer God will definitely answer.[21]

REFLECTION QUESTIONS

1. If you were to make a pie chart of your prayer-life, what percent is spent on petition and intercession, praise and thanksgiving, and surrender

---

20 Frederick Buechner, *Whistling in the Dark: A Doubter's Dictionary* (San Francisco: Harper & Row, 1988), 84.
21 See Reflection Chapter 2 Reflection Question 6.

to God? What kinds of things do you mentions in prayer?
2. What is quid pro quo spirituality? Do you find yourself thinking in these terms? What if more of our prayers were focused on bringing about what God wants instead of what we want?
3. What does Jesus' prayer in the Garden of Gethsemane teach us about prayer?
4. Where is the bottleneck that keeps God's spirit from flowing more freely through your life, family, and church? In what ways might you be part of the bottleneck?
5. What are some of the defining characteristics of the politics of the kingdom of heaven? How can we go about living out God's politics instead of the politics of self-interest?
6. What might have to change in your life if you were to pray the Lord's Prayer more frequently and authentically?

3

Give us this day our daily bread

Whenever I reach this part of the Lord's Prayer, I can almost smell the bread coming out hot from the oven. I have a bread problem. I could never go on the South Beach, Paleo, or Low-Carb diets. I *need* bread. For me there is no finer food in the world than a loaf of warm French bread with butter.

One of my hobbies is baking bread. I have spent the last ten years learning how to make French bread. There is something almost magical about it. It has only four ingredients—flour, water, yeast, and salt—but when prepared properly, it transforms into something completely different—bread. Peter Reinhart, the most famous baker in the world, writes,

> It is difficult for me to discuss going deeply into the process of spiritual unfoldment without also doing so in the context of bread baking, that's how intertwined they have become for me.[22]

There is something deeply spiritual about baking bread, using your bare hands to render a mystical transformation. It is easy to see why Jesus

---

22 Peter Reinhart, *Bread Upon the Water: A Pilgrimage Toward Self-Discovery and Spiritual Truth* (New York: Rodale Books, 2007), 15.

compares the kingdom of heaven to yeast working through a ball of dough (Matthew 13:33). You do not need to be a Christian to know that bread is sacred. Whether it is grandma's biscuits and gravy, your father's Saturday morning pancakes, or the "Hot Donuts" sign at Krispy Kreme—bread is a food that triggers memories.[23]

If we are honest, this is our favorite part of the prayer. We have finally moved to a petition that is about us. In fact, I would suggest that the majority of our prayer life finds its place in this petition. Every time we pray that God meets a need in our life or the lives of others, we are praying for bread. It is a gift in itself that Jesus makes room for our needs in this model prayer. The overarching theme of the prayer is thinking and living beyond ourselves—for God and for others—but Jesus takes time for our concerns. The things that matter to us, no matter how trivial, also matter to God because God loves us. Though we should fill our prayers with more our own wants and needs, we don't have to aim for self-denial. To pray for our needs is not being selfish; it's following Jesus' command.

One of the first things we should note is that praying for bread has a limiting function. Sometimes our prayer life is like a Janis Joplin song:

---

23 See Chapter 3 Reflection Question 1.

> Oh Lord, won't you buy me a Mercedes Benz?
> My friends all drive Porsches,
> I must make amends.
> Worked hard all my lifetime,
> no help from my friends,
> So Lord, won't you buy me a Mercedes Benz?"[24]

When Jesus tells us to pray for "daily bread," he is not saying we should pray for daily filet mignon, daily caviar, or daily lobster tail. We are praying for the most basic food in the world—bread. The notion that Christian prayer is exceedingly spiritual is shattered by this mundane, quotidian prayer for bread.

Bread Is Life

Bread is food for the hungry masses. I live on the Gulf Coast of Florida, and when a hurricane is headed our way, the first thing that runs out at Piggly Wiggly is, you guessed it, the bread. People rush in and fill up their carts with bread. White, wheat, cinnamon raisin—it does not matter. I've always thought this was a little strange. On a regular day, folks pop into the Pig for fried chicken, steamed shrimp, salad fixings, and chips and dips. Put a hurricane in the Gulf of Mexico and everyone is suddenly ravenous for plain white bread.

That should tell us something—bread is life. When we are pushed, when systems are stressed, we fall back on bread. The ancient Sumerians and

---

24 Janis Joplin, "O Lord, Won't You Buy Me a Mercedes Benz?" "Genius" (https://genius.com/Janis-joplin-mercedes-benz-lyrics).

Egyptians were able to build some of the first human civilizations because of bread. The word *culture* finds its roots in *agriculture*. That means all the wonderful aspects of human civilization such as art, music, and philosophy are made possible because of agriculture. It is easy to forget how connected we are to the land. Food does not come from the grocery store, it comes from the earth.

Furthermore, to pray for *us* to have *our* daily bread places Christians in a community with people who are hungry and need food. Bread is the food of the beggar and the salvation of the hungry. Whenever we pray the Lord's Prayer, we join our voices with the poor and cry out for bread. I have long been troubled by an old sermon from St. Basil the Great. He once preached:

> The bread that is spoiling in your house belongs to the hungry. The shoes that are mildewing under you bed belong to those who have none. The clothes stored away in your trunk belong to those who are naked. The money that depreciates in your treasury belongs to the poor![25]

St. Basil's point is that private property is not a Christian category. We have been given what we have in order to bless others. Instead, most of us are like the rich fool of Luke 12, who builds bigger barns to hold his grain for the future, so he can

---

25 Willimon & Hauerwas, 76.

"eat, drink, and be merry." Meanwhile, his soul is being demanded of him. He fails to quote the last part of the verse from Ecclesiastes, "for tomorrow we shall die." To be a Christian is to live focused on eternity and the kingdom of God instead of our short-term well-being.

One strange thing about this petition for bread to "Our Father" is that it is communal. I think we usually mean, "Give me my daily stuff." Yet Jesus is teaching us that when we pray for "our daily bread," we are not just praying for our own needs but for the needs of others. In fact, our needs and the needs of others are all tied up together. In praying the Lord's Prayer, we join the beggar with our hands out, asking for a loaf of bread. Praying these words places us in solidarity with the poor and hungry—certainly not above them or apart from them It opens our hearts to those in need around us.[26]

Furthermore, to pray this prayer is to have friends. Bread is a communal food. The word companion comes from two Latin words, *cum panum*. It means "with bread." Our companions, our family, and friends are people with whom we share bread. To pray for "our bread" is to pray for friendship. The older I get, the more I realize how important it is to have friends. A true friend is a rare gift from God indeed.

I never guessed how involved praying for daily bread could be. In this simple request, so many things are included. In its most basic meaning, it in-

---

26 See Chapter 3 Reflection Question 2.

cludes all that we need for a wholesome existence. Martin Luther made a list in his smaller catechism of all the things that daily bread means. The list is exhaustive: food, drink, clothes, shoes, houses, farms, fields, lands, money, property, a good marriage, good children, honest and faithful public servants, a just government, favorable weather (neither too hot nor too cold), health, honors, good friends, and loyal neighbors.[27] Renowned Swiss Theologian Karl Barth noted that Luther's list contains all that a bourgeois farmer needed in the sixtieth century.[28] The point is that this prayer for daily bread is a prayer for all that we need not simply to *exist* but to *thrive* in our current time and place. Jesus invites us to pray for our most basic needs and the needs of others. God is not too busy or otherwise disposed to be concerned about our worldly struggles. Jesus teaches us that we have a God who is interested in human flourishing. To pray this prayer is to trust that God will provide.[29]

Bread of Heaven

The prayer for bread is first a prayer for real bread—to have our needs met—but theologians and Bible scholars tell us that there is a deeper meaning here. Bread is not just a symbol for the basics of life, it is a symbol for a deep sacramental life. In many places within scripture, we are told there

27 Martin Luther, *Smaller Catechsism*
28 Karl Barth, *Prayer,* 50th Anniversary ed. (Louisville: Westminster John Knox Press, 2022), 46.
29 See Chapter 3 Reflection Question 3.

is a great messianic banquet coming. One day all of our most basic needs will be met, and the Messiah will bring fulfillment to our hunger. Here Barth helps us again:

Bread is something sacred. Bread is the promise, and not only the promise but also the mysterious presence, of this food which nourishes once and for all. Bread is the mysterious presence of this food which, after it has been eaten, does not need to be replaced. In the Bible each meal is sacred, for it is the promise of an eternal banquet, of an everlasting feast.[30]

To pray for daily bread is to ask for the kingdom of God to come. This is made more evident if we look at the original Greek. The Lord's Prayer in Matthew's Gospel has a strange word that we translate as "daily." The word is *epiousios*. It appears nowhere else in scripture, nor is it found in any other ancient source. Therefore, we don't know its exact meaning, but almost all scholars agree that "daily" is a rather random translation. It seems that St. Jerome chose the most literal translation for the Vulgate—the principal Latin version of the Bible—with the word "supersubstantial," with *epi* as a prefix for *super* or *above* and *ousios* meaning *being* or *substance*. This translation gives bread a more spiritual dimension. Other scholars believe it means something like, "Give us today our bread for tomorrow." They find the Greek to be a corruption of the word *epienai,* meaning *tomorrow*. To ask to

---

30   Barth, *Prayer*, 48-49

have tomorrow's bread today is the same as asking for the kingdom to come. N.T. Wright translates it as, "Give us here and now, the bread of life which is promised for the great Tomorrow." What we have here is a prayer for spiritual manna. The bread for which we pray is real bread, but it is also more. This is what Jesus means when he says, "I am the bread of life." It is to acknowledge that we need God's presence in our lives to survive. Our prayer for daily bread does exactly the same thing the Eucharist does. It links our daily life, bread, and survival to *eternal* life. In something as basic as bread, Christ is present to us. In our struggle for survival, God walks with us. Bread is, for Christians, a symbol of our temporal life and our eternal life.[31]

What Is It?

As Christians—all bread, all of life—is manna from heaven. My favorite part of the Exodus story is God's miraculous feeding of the Israelites with manna from heaven. They have no clue what it is, which is why they called it manna. In Hebrew that word means, "What is it?" The Israelites were desperate for sustenance as they wandered in the wilderness to the land flowing with milk and honey—the Promised Land. They cried out for food, and every morning they woke up to a layer of white flaky stuff on the ground. They knew that it came from heaven, but they did not know what it was.

---

31 See Chapter 3 Reflection Question 4.

Give us this day our daily bread 39

Barbara Brown Taylor says that the way God provided manna might have been from the secretion of a desert insect. The Bedouins in the region still eat this substance and still call it manna. What if God miraculously provided for the Hebrew children with bug juice? It definitely changes the way we understand God's blessings.

> If your manna has to drop straight out of heaven looking like a perfect loaf of butter-crust bread, then chances are you are going to go hungry a lot. When the bread you get does not look like the bread you are praying for, you tend to think God is ignoring you, punishing you, or... worse yet...non-existent. Then you start comparing yourself to other people and wondering why they have more to eat...or get more of their prayers answered...than your do. Meanwhile, you miss more of the things that God is doing for you...because they look too ordinary (like bug juice), or too transitory (like manna, which melts the minute the sun gets hot). If on the other hand, you are willing to look at everything that comes to you as coming from God, then there will be no end to the manna in your life. A can of beans will be manna. Grits will be manna...Because it is not what it is that counts but who sent it, and the miracle is that God is always sending us something to eat.[32]

---

32 Barbara Brown Taylor, *The Bread of Angels*, (Norwich: Canterbury Press, 2025), 22.

This is a reminder as we walk through our wilderness—that God's sustenance does not always look like we expect it to look. The Lord might not rain down from heaven perfect buttered loaves of French bread. We have to be more vigilant because most often our first response to God's miracle in our lives is "What is it?" and we will miss God's provisions.[33]

God as Giver

When we pray, "Give us this day our daily bread," we are praying for a lot more than we ever guessed. It is a prayer for our most basic provision, and it is a prayer for the kingdom of heaven. It is a prayer for my lunch and a prayer for the hungry masses around the world.

The prayer has a lot to say about us and our lives, but it's most interesting in what it says about God. And what does this petition say about God? "Give us" is what we pray because we know that God is a giving God. To pray this prayer is to admit that bread is not something we can earn. Life is not something that is achieved. We do not make our own lives; all of life is a gift. As the Epistle of James (1:17) states, "Every good and perfect gift comes from above, coming down from the Father of lights." To pray for bread is to realize that our whole lives are dependent on God's goodness and mercy. We are not and have never been an inde-

---

[33] See Chapter 3 Reflection Question 5.

pendent people. Independence is a great human lie; we are fully and utterly dependent on God.

One of the images of the Christian life I keep coming back to for meaning is the upside-down life of grace. This image is shaped from G. K. Chesterton's telling of the story of St. Francis. Building on Plato's famous allegory of the cave, he says that St. Francis' conversion was as if he came out of a cave walking on his hands and by doing so saw the whole world hanging upside down. That is what *dependence* means—it comes from the Latin meaning "to dangle." Chesterton states, referring to a walled city:

> But the point is this: that whereas to normal eye the large masonry of its walls or the massive foundations of its watch towers and its high citadel would make it seem safer and more permanent, the moment it was turned over the very same weight would make it seem more helpless and more in peril. It is but a symbol; but it happens to fit the psychological fact. ... He might see and love every tile on the steep roofs or every bird on the battlements; but he would see them all in a new and divine light of eternal danger and dependence. Instead of being merely proud of his strong city because it could not be moved, he would be thankful to God Almighty that it had not been dropped; he would be thankful to God for not drop-

ping the whole cosmos like a vast crystal to be shattered into falling stars.[34]

Saint Francis never saw the world the same again. Now, the greatest symbols of strength, the great towers of government and church, just seem to barely hang on by a hair, and everything was dependent on God. Before his conversion, Frances saw the world as we see it: trees and towers and people, and after his conversion, he saw everything the same way, but exactly opposite. Instead of everything weighted down to earth, he saw it all upside down, dangling from God's hand. To pray for God "to give us this day our daily bread" is to see the world in a revolutionary way; it is to see everything hanging precariously on the grace and mercy of God. If grace is the theme of the universe then we must see the world upside-down like Francis.

To pray the Lord's Prayer is to see God as the giver of all life. It is to know that even the smallest aspect of life, like bread, is grace. For Christians, grace is the foundation for everything. To pray for "daily bread" is to ask for salvation by grace alone, and this gets to the root of the Christian life. Because salvation and all of life is a gift, the only response that we have is thanksgiving. This is why the mystic Meister Eckhart, says, "If the only prayer you ever say in your life is 'thank you,' that would suffice."[35]

---

34 G. K. Chesterton, *St. Francis of Assisi* (Mineola, NY: Dover Publications, 2008), 60—61.

35 Meister Eckart cited from Anne Lamott, *Help, Thanks, Wow*, (Westminster, Maryland: Riverhead Books, 2012).

Our ability to give thanks to God in all circumstances is directly proportional to our understanding of grace and salvation. Praying for "daily bread" forms a people who see God as the Great Giver and all of life as an occasion for thanksgiving.[36]

REFLECTION QUESTIONS

1. What kind of bread triggers your memories? What does it bring to mind?
2. How does understanding that the Lord's Prayer places us in solidarity with the poor transform the way we live?
3. Using Luther's expanded definition of "daily bread," which includes extras that create a comfortable life in our world, what kind of things—a living wage, Internet access, home ownership—are on our list today?
4. In what ways is praying to receive bread also praying to receive Christ? How does the Eucharist relate to the Lord's Prayer?
5. What is the manna you are missing because you are looking for perfectly buttered slices of French bread? Have you ever had to ask, "What is it?" after receiving a blessing?
6. What is the connection between asking God to give us bread and giving thanks? How is thanksgiving tied directly to understanding Christian salvation?

---

36 See Chapter 3, Reflection, Question 6.

4

Forgive us our trespasses as we forgive those who trespass against us

We are now moving to the most difficult petition of the prayer—the most painful part. Jesus encourages us to ask for forgiveness and to forgive. This might be the most challenging command in the Bible. A church council record of a Swiss Church tells of a man who pretended not to know the Lord's Prayer simply because he knew that if he prayed it, he would have to forgive the merchant who had cheated him. The man had no plan to forgive his offender and was honest enough not to pray the prayer. Most of us are not that honest. Instead of pretending we don't know the prayer, we pretend that we do not understand it. Mark Twain's famous quip reflects our attitude best: "It ain't the parts of the Bible I don't understand that bother, it is the parts I do understand."[37] Unfortunately, we understand exactly what Jesus is saying.

This kind of prayer does not come naturally to us as human beings. The national media struggled to comprehend the radical forgiveness shown by the Amish Christian community. In October 2006, a man named Charles Roberts entered a one-room

---

37 Mark Twain / 1835-1910 / in Alex Ayres, *The Wit and Wisdom, of Mark Twain*, 1987.

schoolhouse in Nickel Mines, Pennsylvania. He shot ten young girls, killing five, before taking his own life. It was a horrific, senseless act of violence.

But what happened next shocked the world. That very day, members of the Amish community visited Roberts's widow. They offered words of forgiveness. They embraced her. They brought food to her home. Just a few days later, more than half of those who attended the gunman's funeral were Amish. They mourned not only their own children but also the lost soul of the man who had taken them.

Their forgiveness was not naive. It was not a way of avoiding grief. It was an act of faith—quiet, unwavering, and deeply surprising to nearly everyone watching.

This was also the case in June 2015 during the days following the massacre at Mother Emanuel African Methodist Episcopal Church in Charleston, South Carolina. An act of terror, committed by a young man in the name of white Christian nationalism against a group of black Christians in prayer, left nine people dead. The nation was stunned and angry, but Mother Emanuel AME did not respond with a thirst for vengeance. Instead, one by one, many of the victims' relatives forgave the man for killing their innocents. Some even said they did not wish to see him sentenced to death. The American media did not know what to do with this story. It was like they discovered an endangered species.

Maybe what that massacre shows us is that true Christians are a rare find.[38]

Forgiveness does not come naturally to human beings. We hold grudges, we make lists of faults, and we love being victims. We wear victimhood like a badge of honor, signaling to everyone that we have been wronged. The manner in which we consume the news in our country seems to perpetuate even greater victimhood by constantly reminding us we have been wronged by foreign groups, past events, or our own government. It's as if our society believes these wounds must remain fresh, never allowed to heal. A friend of mine says the mantra of the news today is, "Aren't you mad about this?" Our cable news culture seems bent on nurturing these grievances, the bulk of which are manufactured. Still, there is a lot to be mad about in this world. There is plenty of real injury, and it is completely human to crave justice or even vengeance.

For Christians, however, these white-hot desires are tempered by God's uncommon love and mercy. In his prayer on that mountain, Jesus shows us another way. He shows us God's justice and it is centered on the cross. Paul tells us that the cross is God's justice and righteousness. In light of this great fact, Christianity teaches us to pray daily for forgiveness. There is nothing more counter-cultural or more difficult to do than to pray for forgiveness. Jesus teaches us to pray, "Forgive us our trespasses as we forgive those who trespass against

---

38 See Chapter 4 Reflection Question 1.

us." Trespass is word that has fallen out of use, but its most basic meaning is a violation. It's another way of referring to our wrongdoings, our sins.

The Economy, Stupid!

This is a prayer of confession. Our Presbyterian brothers and sisters say the great prayer a bit differently, asking, "Forgive us our debts." A wise Presbyterian once told me, "Any Presbyterian knows it is better to have your debts forgiven than your trespasses." *Trespasses* is the traditional language of the church, but *debts* gets closer to the heart of the matter. What we are talking about here is not something that is overtly spiritual; we are talking about economics.

How important is economics? The wild and controversial political consultant, James Carvel, famously quipped, "It's the economy, stupid." That classic piece of political shorthand is used to explain why some people jettison their closely held views and opinions on issues foreign and domestic when the economy is in trouble. Straight out the window. Because there's really only one concern—the economy. Economics explains a lot. Many authors, like Steven Levitt and Stephen Dubner of *Freakonomics* (2005), have sought to show how economic factors color everything.

When we look at Jesus' mission statement from his first sermon (Luke 4), we see a very economic message. He preached from Isaiah 61 about the restoration of the Jubilee—the year of the Lord's favor. His gospel was to bring good news to the poor and to release debts. The Greek word used in the Gospels for forgiveness is *aphesis*. This is the word used in the Septuagint to refer to the Jubilee. The core of Jesus' message was forgiveness—both financial and spiritual.

Many economists today say that after the great recession ended we have two economies. The first economy has recovered. In fact, it is at an all-time high with the stock market at peak. The second economy, however, is still in recession with slow job growth and low wages. Economists tell us our spending habits and other behaviors differ widely, depending on which economy you live in.

Thinking about economics this way is helpful in understanding Jesus' prayer. Jesus is telling us that there is another economy—God's economy. The word economy comes from two Greek words, *oikos* and *nomos*, meaning house law. Jesus shows us how it works in God's house. In our human households, which are based on scarcity, market forces and merit drive the economy, but in God's house, where abundance abounds, different forces reign.

When Jesus tells us to pray for debts to be forgiven, he is inviting us to live in this new economy. First of all, this economy begins with our debts. Jesus teaches that every human being is in great debt to God. We owe God a debt that we cannot even begin to repay. We are in default. In fact, that is how the French translate trespasses—faults. We are in default with God. Wouldn't it be so much better for us if the great prayer just read, "Teach us to be forgiving people"? I am afraid that this is what we usually mean when we pray the prayer. Instead, it begins by implicating us as debtors in default with God. We cannot start with forgiveness of our neighbors until we first realize that we are a guilty party. None of us, no matter how good we think we are, can skate by this judgment. That is why Christians are not primarily victims, but instead first and foremost perpetrators. We are spiritually and morally bankrupt. This is a difficult and painful place to be, but Jesus clearly teaches us this is where the human condition begins.

First, we acknowledge that we are in default and bankrupt. Then we beg for forgiveness. From an earthly perspective, it's a dire, even hopeless situation. Christians know otherwise. The good news of the gospel is that God in Christ Jesus has forgiven us. Despite our debts and despite our guilt, we have been bailed out. We have been saved, and the debt has been forgiven.[39] Then Jesus moves to an even more difficult place. The prayer says, "Forgive us our debts *as* we forgive those who have debts against us." With those words, our debts to God are inextricably linked to others' debts to us. And not only our sins but our forgiveness as well. The forgiveness we seek from God is linked to the forgiveness we grant those "who trespass against us."

This might be the hardest passage in the prayer because it takes away our claim to victimhood. As

---

39 See Chapter 4 Reflection Question 2.

God's debtor, we have just lost our place of power, and now we must turn to our neighbors and forgive. I have always been troubled by this little word *as*. Is Jesus insinuating we won't be forgiven by God if we cannot forgive our neighbors? Do we really know what we are praying? Do I really want God to forgive me as I forgive others? No, I want God to forgive me despite my inability to forgive. But Jesus does not let us off the hook that easily.

God's forgiveness to us is free—it is grace and not granted based on anything we do. It is not even determined by our forgiveness of others. God's forgiveness of our sins comes first. But here in this prayer Jesus links the two. My sister pointed out to me that this part of the prayer reminds her of Jesus' Golden Rule: "Do unto others as you would have them do unto you." (Matthew 7:12) I had never equated the two, but now I see the connection. We should forgive others as we want to be forgiven.

Jesus, in what might be his most challenging parable, gives us the story of the unmerciful servant in Matthew 18. A servant owes a king a great sum of money—a myriad of *denarii*. An ungodly amount of money—the largest conceivable in the ancient world—it is meant to be almost a joke. It would be like us saying someone owed the government the entire national debt. As of this writing, the national debt is over twenty trillion dollars. I have no frame of reference to understand a debt this large. But the king brought him in and somehow forgave the whole thing! The entire national debt was wiped out and forgotten. But then the servant remembered he had a friend who owed him a few hundred bucks. What did the servant do? He shook his friend down and demanded that the man pay up immediately.

The friend begged the servant for mercy but found none. He was thrown into debtor's prison. Soon the king heard about this and summoned the servant. Jesus tells us, "Then the master called the servant in. 'You wicked servant,' he said, 'I canceled all that debt of yours because you begged me to. Shouldn't you have had mercy on your fellow servant just as I had on you?'" In anger, his master handed him over to the jailers to be tortured until he could pay back all he owed—which of course he could never do. The message of the parable is the same as the great prayer. Our forgiveness of the sins of others is linked—or should be linked— to God's forgiveness of our sins.

The prayer invites us to live in a different economy where debts are forgiven, an economy of grace. To live in this economy is to view the entire world as a gift. To live in the economy of forgiveness and mercy is to live in a drastically different world. Once mercy has been extended to you, you cannot help but to extend it to others. [40]

Healing and Reconciliation

Maybe you have been wronged by someone in a way that you just cannot get over. Maybe you have

---

[40] See Chapter 4 Reflection Question 3.

an enemy that you just cannot love. What's the answer? I have had people in my life I could not forgive. Anger burned within me for the offenses they had committed against me. I carried those offenses everywhere I went, and, at times, I allowed them to control my life. In reality, they were relatively minor. As a white man living in the richest country in the world, I have experienced little hardship. What about those who have suffered great injury—whether physical or emotional—at the hands of others? What about those who are victims of domestic abuse or war crimes or drunk driving or violent street crimes? How do those people move from trauma and betrayal to forgiveness and healing?

On this matter, I have been profoundly influenced by Archbishop Desmond Tutu, who led the people of South Africa in a process of national healing after apartheid—the systematic oppression of people of color by the wealthy and powerful white minority—was dismantled. The black Africans had suffered horrendously under the white Afrikaners, and when apartheid ended, many expected a blood bath. A response similar to the French Revolution that would repay wrongs and mete out punishments.

But Tutu had a different plan. He knew that justice would only serve to destroy the South African economy and set back the country for decades. Dreaming of a nation shaped by the Gospel, Tutu implemented a system of national reconciliation through which forgiveness could be achieved, and in time, his Truth and Reconciliation Commission brought healing to his deeply divided country.

We often hear that forgiveness is forgetting. Tutu tells us otherwise:

> Forgiving is not forgetting; it's actually remembering—remembering and not using your right to hit back. It's a second chance for a new beginning. And the remembering part is particularly important. Especially if you don't want to repeat what happened.[41]

Forgiveness is not forgetting but remembering. When we ask God to forgive us, we confess our sins. In confession, we acknowledge the truth about ourselves. We remember our sins, and in remembering them, God forgives us and God remembers them no more. Tutu helps us further understand:

> Forgiving and being reconciled to our enemies or our loved ones are not about pretending that things are other than they are. It is not about patting one another on the back and turning a blind eye to the wrong. True reconciliation exposes the awfulness, the abuse, the hurt, the truth. It could even sometimes make things worse. It is a risky undertaking, but in the end, it is worthwhile, because in the end only an honest confrontation with reality can bring real

---

41 Desmond Tutu, *No Future Without Forgiveness* (New York: Doubleday, 1999), 270-271.

healing. Superficial reconciliation can bring only superficial healing. [42]

God does not want superficial reconciliation from us. Deep healing comes from remembering what happened and telling the story of our injury and then, despite that, extending forgiveness to those who have wronged us.[43]

Extending this forgiveness is good not just for the offender but for the offended. Harboring anger and injury only further adds insult to our injury. Tutu points out that it's actually in our best interest to forgive:

> Thus, to forgive is indeed the best form of self-interest since anger, resentment, and revenge are corrosive of that *summum bonum*, that greatest good, communal harmony that enhances the humanity and personhood of all in the community.[44]

But in our state of injury this is hard to see, and a prolonged resistance to forgiveness and reconciliation can eat us up from the inside and destroy our life from within.

Rabbi Harold Kushner tells a helpful story in his article, "Letting Go of the Role of Victim":

---

42 Ibid, 271.
43 See Chapter 4 Reflection Question 4
44 Ibid, 270-271.

> A woman in my congregation comes to see me. She is a single mother, divorced, working to support herself and three young children. She says to me, "Since my husband walked out on us, every month is a struggle to pay our bills. I have to tell my kids we have no money to go to the movies while he's living it up with his new wife in another state. How can you tell me to forgive him?" I answer her, "I'm asking you to forgive him because he doesn't deserve the power to live in your head and turn you into a bitter, angry woman. I'd like to see him out of your life emotionally as completely as he is out of it physically, but you keep holding on to him. You're not hurting him by holding on to that resentment, but you're hurting yourself.[45]

We need to let go of the resentment that we have toward our offenders, not just for their sake but for ours. It is so easy to let our lives be defined by our enemies and their actions, but we must not let them have that power. Mark Twain once said, "Anger is the acid that does more damage to the vessel in which it is stored than on anything it is poured." Anger and resentment only deepens and exacerbates our injury.[46]

Not only does forgiveness give the injured individual a way forward—it is also is the only way for communities to move forward. Our communal history is one filled with atrocities from the treatment

---

45 Kushner, Harold S., "Letting Go of the Role of Victim," *Spirituality and Health*, Winter 1999, 34.
46 See Chapter 4 Reflection Question 5.

of native people to the institution of slavery, and beyond. The only way for our communities to move forward is with the hard work of forgiveness—telling the truth about our past and making reconciliation.

Our communal future rest on our ability to forgive, and followers of Jesus must lead the way. We must, in every community, have our own Truth and Reconciliation Commission. It is time to tear down our walls and build bridges in our families, churches, communities, and nation. To pray for forgiveness is to pray for the kingdom of God to come.

Forgiveness is at the center of the Christian faith because in Jesus, we find forgiveness from God. Paul tells us in Romans that Christ proves his love toward us in this: "While we were yet sinners Christ died for us." We are the people who put Jesus on the cross, but while hanging on that cross, he prayed for us, "Father, forgive them for they know not what they do." To be a Christian is to receive this forgiveness from Christ whom we have harmed. But it is also to offer that same forgiveness to those we have harmed and ask for forgiveness when we have harmed others. How many times should we offer forgiveness to the one who offended us? Peter recommended seven times, but Jesus came back with seven times seventy (Matthew 18:22)! In other words, we are to forgive in the measure that God has forgiven us. That measure is inexhaustible. [47]

---

47 See Chapter 4 Reflection Question 6.

REFLECTION QUESTIONS

1. What story of forgiveness from the news or your life experience has inspired you?
2. How does God's economy differ from our earthly economy?
3. What is Jesus trying to teach us in the Parable of the Unmerciful Servant?
4. Why is remembering a crucial part of forgiveness? Why can we just let bygones be bygones and forget our past?
5. In what ways does withholding forgiveness add more harm to the injured?
6. What would it look like for our nation to have a Truth and Reconciliation Commission? What are other ways for deep healing and reconciliation to occur between people of different races, religions, socioeconomic statuses, or political beliefs?

5

Lead us not into temptation but deliver us from evil

Axis of Evil

Now we near the end of the great prayer with its final petition. I would argue it is the petition we ignore most, usually praying it as an afterthought. The first part of the petition is for God to lead us. To be led by Christ is the core of what Christians are called to do. Consider the way Jesus called the disciples. He did not say, "Believe in me." He did not say, "Live like me." Instead, everywhere he went, he said, "Follow me."

Lead Us!

A Christian is not first and foremost a person who has a static set of belief or practices. A Christian is a person who follows Christ. The trouble with following Jesus is that he is always on the move. At many times in my spiritual journey, I believed that I had come to a resting place. There's really no such thing when it comes to living as a disciple of Christ. Furthermore, just because you decided to follow him long ago does not mean you are still following him now. Just look at the Gospels: Bethlehem, Egypt, Nazareth, Capernaum, Gentile territories, and Jerusalem. He never stops moving. For us, that means following Jesus is a daily decision; Christ calls us to constant conversion.

To be a Christian means to follow Jesus—wherever Jesus will take you, and Jesus always takes you to unexpected places. Abram had to leave his family and his country and journey to an unknown land. When the disciples followed Jesus, they could not have known how much the journey was going to cost them—their very lives. It is highly unlikely in our current American context that God is calling us to die for him, but he is calling us to live for him, which might be just as hard. Jesus says if you want to be his disciples you must, "Take up your cross, deny yourself and follow me." Following Jesus means losing your life—but in losing it, you find it. Dietrich Bonhoeffer, a theologian and pastor executed by Adolf Hitler, once said, "When Jesus calls a man he bids him come and die."[48] Being led by Jesus means we go places we might not want to go.

A haunting story comes to mind whenever I think that I am following Jesus. A farmer named Clarence Jordan showed the world what it is like to actually be church. He had a transformational moment when he invited a Native American man to his church one Sunday, but the deacons stopped him at the door and said, "You can't bring him in here." Jordan responded, "Show me where it says that in the Bible." They could not find it anywhere but still barred the man from entering. It was then that Jordan felt called by God to start a communi-

---

48 Bonhoeffer, *Cost of Discipleship*.

ty—a Christian farming community near Americus, Georgia—a church where all of God's children could worship no matter their skin color, nationality, or political views. Jordan called it Koinonia Farms.

The neighbors did not like it. They burned crosses in his front yard, threw bricks through the windows, and sued him for breaking segregation laws. None of that stopped Jordan would not stop following Jesus. He once asked his brother, Robert, who became a state senator and a justice on the Georgia Supreme Court, to be Koinonia's attorney. His brother replied, "I can't do that. You know my aspirations. I might lose my job, my house, everything I've got." Clarence said, "We might lose everything, too." "It's different for you," Robert responded. Then Clarence replied, "Why? You and I joined the church the same Sunday as boys. The preacher asked, 'Do you accept Jesus as your Lord and Savior?' What did you say?" Robert replied, "I follow Jesus — up to a point." Clarence said, "Could that point by any chance be the cross?" "I follow him to the cross, but not on the cross. I'm not getting myself crucified," Robert replied. Clarence answered, "Then I don't believe you are a disciple. You're an admirer of Jesus. You ought to go back to that church you belong to, and tell them you're an admirer, not a disciple."[49]

---

49 James Wm. McClendon Jr., "The Theory Tested: Clarence Leonard Jordan — Radical in Community," in *Biography as Theology: How Life Stories Can Remake Today's Theology* (Philadelphia: Trinity Press International, 1990), 103.

Most of us would gladly follow Jesus up to a point. We can gather around the fire at church camp and sing, "I have decided to follow Jesus," but I fear that what we actually do is admire Jesus from a safe distance. In the Lord's Prayer, when we say, "Lead us not into temptation," first and foremost we are praying to be led.[50]

Temptation

When we ask not to be led into temptation it is not as if God would lead us into our temptation. James 1:3 tells us, "When tempted, no one should say, 'God is tempting me.' For God cannot be tempted by evil, nor does he tempt anyone." With this petition, we are asking God to lead us *out* of temptation. It's a powerful act, placing your life in the hands of the Almighty. In 2017, Pope Francis controversially recommended a change in translation of the Lord's Prayer to "Do not let us fall into temptation." He was chiefly worried that because of the normal translation people would get the idea that it is God who leads us into temptation. However, that is not what the prayer is stating. It is the evil one who leads us into temptation and God who leads us out.

This petition is complementary to the one for daily bread. That petition asks God to give us good things. This petition runs counter to that notion, asking God to take away evil. They fit together as two different sides of the same coin. John Wesley's

---

50 See Chapter 5 Reflection Question 1.

first two rules of life mirror this. He said first, "Do no harm" and second, "Do good." They are two separate commands that ultimately get you to the same place. Yet this prayer for deliverance from evil is asking for far more than simply the removal of bad things. Here we are talking about evil—and not just evil as a category. The Greek text should be rendered here as, "Deliver us from the *evil one*." We are talking about the devil. Most of us moderns seldom think about the devil.

Done with the Devil?

I once was accosted after church one Sunday because I chose the hymn, "A Mighty Fortress Is Our God." This great hymn of the church was written by Martin Luther himself. I asked, "What is wrong with the hymn?" The problem, according to a small group of people gathered in my study, is that it talks too much about the devil: "For still our ancient foe doth seek to work us woe, his wrath and power are great" as well as "And though the world with devils filled still threatens to undo us." The leader of this group looked at me and said, "Every verse of the song had something to do with the devil. Aren't we past this? Aren't we done with the devil?" I replied, "Maybe you are done with the devil, but I am still having trouble with him." At times, I suppose I agree with her sentiment. But I also think Frederick Buechner was right when he said,

> To take the Devil seriously is to take seriously the fact that the total evil in the world is greater than the sum of all its parts. Likewise, the total evil in yourself. The murderer who says, "I couldn't help it," isn't necessarily just kidding.[51]

I don't think that praying to be delivered from the evil one requires us to believe in a little red man with horns and pitch fork who lives in the center of the earth. It is to admit that the evil forces in the world are more than just what is in each individual's heart. There are larger forces that Saint Paul calls principalities and powers.

When I began to study the Lord's Prayer in depth, I was talking to my father about this endeavor. I never quite know what my father, a retired neuroscientist, is thinking when it comes to religion, but I was surprised when he said that the one petition he wanted to know about the most was evil. He said, "I want to be delivered from evil." I was surprised because I, like many modern people, seem to have trouble with the theology of evil. I was prepared to tell him that C. S. Lewis once pointed out there is no reference to the devil in any of the three Christian creeds—and therefore entirely possible to be a Christian without believing in the devil.[52] However, my father found it very easy to believe in evil. I suppose it does not take a lot of faith to believe in

---

51 Originally published in *Wishful Thinking* and later in *Beyond Words*

52 C.S. Lewis, *God in the Dock*, "Answers to Questions about Christianity"(1944), pp. 56-57.

evil. We see it all the time. There are forces at work that are so dark and destructive that evil is the only explanation.

A line in the movie *The Usual Suspects* says, "The greatest trick the devil ever pulled was convincing the world he didn't exist." That would be tricky indeed. To deny evil's work in the world begins by denying the basic teaching that we have in Genesis: that humankind is created in the image of God and called good by God.

In *The Screwtape Letters*, C.S. Lewis tells us,

> there are two equal and opposite errors into which our race can fall about devils. One is to disbelieve in the existence. The other is to believe, and to feel an excessive and unhealthy interests in them. They themselves are equally pleased with both errors and hail a materialist or a magician with the same delight.[53]

We must be careful not to focus too much or too little on evil. I have been part of Christian circles that saw devils working in everything. It is easy to be like Flip Wilson of Saturday Night Live and say, "The devil made me do it" about everything. The Orthodox teaching of the church does not think that good and evil are equal and opposite forces like Manicheists. Compared to the goodness of God, the devil and all the endless forms of evil are nothing. The old saying goes that we must "give the devil his

---

53 C.S. Lewis, *Screwtape Letters*, preface.

due." There is truth in this. We must not become complacent and forget that evil has us surrounded, but sometimes the church makes the devil a demigod with the power and ability to be everywhere. This is clearly much more power than he is due.[54]

When you turn on the news and hear about terrorism and ISIS, you see evil at work. It is all too easy to see evil at play in our enemies. However, Jesus' prayer does not let us get off that easy. It makes clear that temptation and evil just as present among his followers, and throughout history we can see that evil is often most strong with people of faith. Those outside of faith don't face the same struggles with evil as those inside the faith. The TV preacher will tell you that if you become a Christian, life will get easier for you: things will start looking up. That is partly true, but there is more to the story. Becoming a Christian means that you will face evil like you never have before. In fact, the scriptures tell us there is a war waging between good and evil. To be a Christian means to plunge right into the front lines of this battle. In fact, to be a Christian means that you are the battlefield!

Jesus did battle with the devil right before he entered into his ministry. He was tempted three times while he was in the wilderness for forty days. It was an epic battle. The devil was trying to give Jesus three things that Jesus wanted. They were good things. They were things God wanted Jesus to have, but in time. The devil offered a shortcut, using scrip-

---

[54] See Chapter 4 Reflection Question 2

ture all the way. Like the line in *To Kill a Mockingbird*, sometimes the Bible in the hand of one man is worse that a whiskey bottle in the hand of another.[55] That is the trouble with real temptation. It can look good, even holy. Some of the people behind the most evil moments in history did not think that they were participating in evil. Many of the people who pulled the lever in the gas chambers of the concentration camps in Germany thought they were being good, patriotic Christians. Many of the slave owners across the South legitimately believed that they were helping in some way and following the Bible. Many terrorists believed they were doing God's will by killing innocent civilians. In each case, they were deceived, and very few could see the evil. Fortunately for us, the evil we face is not usually as dramatic as in those instances, but it is still there.

Barbara Brown Taylor says that most of us do not face as big of a challenge:

> When it's our turn, none of us is going to get the Son of God test. We're going to get the regular old Adam and Eve test, which means that the devil won't need much more than an all-you-can-eat buffet and a tax refund to turn our heads.[56]

---

55   Harper Lee, *To Kill a Mocking Bird*.
56   Barbara Brown Taylor, "The Wilderness Exam," Day1, accessed August 4, 2025, https://day1.org/weekly-broadcast/5d9b820ef-71918cdf2002924/the_wilderness_exam.

I suppose we each have our price, and usually it is rather low. The wisdom of the ancient church—particularly its acknowledgement of the *seven deadly sins*—helps us better see temptation in our lives. Those sins were pride, envy, gluttony, lust, anger, greed, and sloth. Sometimes fear is even added to this list. St. Augustine taught that all of these temptations are based on love that is misdirected. Love of people can be turned to lust, enjoyment of food turns to gluttony, healthy love of self becomes pride, and so on. It's tricky because real temptation initially seems so good and holy.

We face temptation and evil in small ways every day, but the kind of evil we are asking to be delivered from is not just our bad habits and foibles, and not the kind of thing we have control over. In the Lord's Prayer, we are asking for deliverance and help because it is outside of our control. Evil is stronger than we are. Barth says that this evil is "stronger than our strength, more clever than our intelligence (including the intelligence we put into our theology), and more dangerously sentimental—for the Devil is also sentimental—than we ourselves are capable of being. He is more pious (yes, the Devil is pious too) than all our Christian piety, both ancient and modern, or theological."[57] We are outmatched, and we cannot withstand the assault on our own.

---

[57] Karl Barth, *Prayer*, 50th Anniversary ed. (Louisville: Westminster John Knox Press, 2022), 62.

Barth tells us that this prayer for deliverance from evil is not really for minor temptations and small sins. Those battles are easy. Those are in our control, and we need to struggle with our sins to grow. For most of our temptations, the devil hardly needs to be involved because we are naturally prone to do bad things and don't need the help of evil. What we are praying for, in the Lord's Prayer, is the big temptation—the one that is a threat to our existence, the temptation that we cannot see. Maybe the most troubling and terrifying scripture of all is 2 Corinthians 11:14 where St. Paul tells us that the devil "masquerades as an angel of light." That is the trouble with true evil. It is so bad because it looks so holy and good, and we cannot sense the danger at all. Our only hope is that God will deliver us. True temptation cannot be beaten by willpower; it can be beaten only by deliverance.[58]

That is why the vows that we make in baptism are so important. Each time we baptize, we take vows that are from the early church. "Do you renounce the spiritual forces of wickedness and reject the evil powers of this world? Will you resist evil, injustice, and oppression in whatever forms they present themselves?" That last part is key because evil won't always manifest as we're expecting. As Bob Dylan warns in his 1979 hit "Gotta Serve Somebody"—"You're gonna have to serve somebody, well, it may be the devil or it may be the Lord, but you're gonna have to serve somebody"—our

---

58   See Chapter 4 Reflection Question 3.

choices are critical. But to be baptized is to have God's power to resist the evil found in the world and in our lives in whatever form it takes.

Jesus teaches us to pray this prayer for deliverance because the first step is admitting that we have a problem and cannot solve it by ourselves. This is the power of the first three steps in any twelve-step program such as Alcoholics Anonymous. Some psychologists have criticized the program because they think that our problems can be solved by sheer willpower and personal striving, but I would argue that AA works because it tells the truth. Against evil—true evil —we are powerless with no hope on our own. We need a higher power. We need God to fix our problems. That is the way we fight evil—not by sheer force of will power but by humbly admitting we need God. Evil is such a strong force that we can face it only with God's power. That is why we pray, "Lead us not into temptation but deliver us from evil."

Martin Luther's song confesses, "Did we in our own strength confide, our striving would be losing." There is nothing that we ourselves can do to flee from temptation. There is not rope strong enough to hold us back nor ear plugs that can drown out the siren's song. The great hymn goes on to say, "Were not the right man on our side, the man of God's own choosing." That is the answer—only God through Jesus Christ gives us the power to resist evil. And the scriptures promise us that if we "resist the devil, he will flee (James 4:7)." That is all that it takes in the power of Christ—a little resistance, and we are free.

A More Beautiful Song

The devil is a seductive creature. One of the most powerful illustrations of temptation is Homer's sirens in his epic tale of the Odyssey. These sirens were irresistibly beautiful, and they were deadly. Ships would sail by and hear them singing their beautiful music and the sailors would jump from their ships to their deaths. There are two mythic heroes who resisted the sirens' songs. The first was Odysseus, who knew of their power and poured wax in his sailors' ears and tied himself to the ship's mast so he could not escape. It worked, but it was not easy.

The person in Greek mythology who conquered the sirens best was Orpheus. He did not pour wax in his ears or tie himself down. Instead, as the sirens began singing, he took out his lyre and played a more beautiful song, drowning out their seductive voices.

I think that is the best description of how Jesus overcomes the devil. He simply plays a more beautiful song.

It reminds me of "The Devil Went Down to Georgia," that classic tune from The Charlie Daniel's Band. With fire flying from his fingertips, the devil plays impressively, but then Johnny show him how it's done. Bowing his head, the devil realizes he's been beat and lays his golden fiddle at Johnny's feet. That's what Jesus does. He outplays the devil every time, and we beat temptation by joining in the more beautiful song.

In Luke 22, Jesus tell Peter that the devil wants to sift Peter like wheat, but Jesus reassures him that he is praying for Peter and that his faith may not fail. If you are a Christian, you will face evil. Evil is out there, and evil is right here. If you think you can handle it on your own, you are badly mistaken. You are in over your head, and you will be swallowed up. The good news is that Jesus prays for you. Jesus has gone head to head with the evil one and prevailed. On the cross, evil in all its many forms was defeated. Jesus is praying for us. He will give us the strength that we need so that our faith will not fail.

The scriptures say that the "devil prowls around like a roaring lion waiting for someone to devour (1 Peter 5:8)." That is a terrifying image of our helplessness. Here the Greek word for *deliver*— *rhýomai*—helps us understand what Christ has done for us. It means to snatch out from the jaws. To be delivered is to belong to Christ and be saved from the jaws of evil. Salvation from evil is just like salvation from our sins; it all comes down to grace. Resisting evil and temptation is not a matter of trying harder or building up more willpower but of following Christ and submitting to his will.[59]

---

59 See Chapter 4 Reflection Question 4.

REFLECTION QUESTIONS

1. Why did Jesus ask us to follow him before he asks us to believe? Where do you think Jesus is asking you to follow him?
2. Have you experienced too much or too little focus on the devil? If we gave the "devil his due," what would his "due" be?
3. What do you think it means that the devil comes "as an angle of light?"
4. Why is it that we are often our most evil when we believe we are doing good?
5. How do Christians resist evil and temptation? Why is willpower not enough?

6

For Thine is the kingdom, the power, and the glory, forever

Now we arrive at the conclusion of the Lord's Prayer. Kingdom, power, glory—these are strong words. This part of the prayer has a musical quality. In fact, there is some indication that it was meant to be sung or chanted. In Albert Hay Malotte's version of the Lord's Prayer, which is frequently sung at weddings and funerals, these words soar into the air with majesty and reach their zenith at *forever*.

For many of us, this grand finale is our favorite part of the prayer. Yet these are not the words that Christ "hath taught us." In truth, these words are not from scripture. They have been added by the church to give the prayer a more formal ending. This might come as a shock to you, if you grew up reading these words in your King James Bible. But our most ancient and most reliable manuscripts from the early church do not include the text. Furthermore, this concluding petition is not in Matthew's or Luke's versions of the Lord's Prayer, and it does not seem to be in the manuscripts that were canonized at Nicaea. Therefore, it is not scripture.

So should we use this concluding petition? Many have said it is better to leave it alone and go only with scripture. They have a strong case, but it would be a shame to lose this ancient conclusion. It belongs with the prayer that our Lord taught us for three reasons.

First, it is tradition. This addition is an ancient one. The first time the Lord's Prayer is mentioned outside of the Bible is in the *Didache*, which dates to around 100 AD. In this most ancient prayer book, we find the Lord's Prayer with this full conclusion. Also, many of the ancient readings of the text contain the long ending. What this shows us is how the early church used the full prayer. We would do well to follow in their footsteps. Using this conclusion gives us a strong connection to the early church.

Second, this final phrase is not just another petition like the others—but a doxology. It seems that the church decided that the prayer needed a proper ending. A doxology frames a prayer and gives it focus or a frame through which to view it. When we add the "Gloria Patri" to the end of a Psalm, we are placing a Hebrew prayer into the full Christian context of the Triune God. When we add a doxology to a creed, we take our ancient statement of faith and make it a prayer. Therefore, when we add a doxology to the Lord's Prayer we are highlighting what the prayer says about God and God's victory in the world.

The third and final reason we should keep this doxology is that it provides a summary of the entire prayer, cutting to the heart of what the prayer is all about. Karl Barth states:

> These final words encompass the whole prayer. The thought would be thus: It is necessary for us to pray, because to thee belongs the kingdom, the power, and the glory, and not to us, human beings.[60]

This entire doxology, which reminds us the prayer is solely about God,[61] hangs on the word *Thine*, a possessive pronoun referring to *our father*. These things—kingdom, power, and glory—all belong to God. It is easy to forget that this prayer is about God because we tend to make it about ourselves. We pray for *our* daily bread, *our* trespasses, and *our* deliverance from evil, but the final doxology reminds us that we are able to ask for these things only because of God and God's greater glory.

These words are powerful, and we must not assume that we know what these words mean simply because we use them frequently. In many ways, "the kingdom, the power, and the glory" have become part of our "Christianese." We have turned them into spiritual words, but first and foremost these are political words. To speak these words is to speak of revolution. Hauerwas and Willimon say that when we pray this part of the Lord's Prayer, "the folks at City Hall ought to get nervous."[62] What

---

60 Karl Barth, *Prayer*, 50th Anniversary ed. (Louisville: Westminster John Knox Press, 2022), 65
61 See Chapter 6 Reflection Question 1.
62 William H. Willimon and Stanley Hauerwas, *Lord, Teach Us: The Lord's Prayer and the Christian Life* (Nashville: Abingdon Press, 1996), 97.

we are talking about here has real-world implications. Luke's Gospel illustrates this by starting its stories with the major political players of the time. For instance, the Christmas story happened while Quirinius was governor of Syria and Tiberius was the emperor of the world. That is what kingdom, power, and glory looked like in the ancient world and still looks like today. And yet the gospel unfolded in the backwaters of Galilee with an unmarried pregnant young woman. The song (Luke 1:46-55) that she sang should give us a clue: "My soul magnifies the Lord, my spirit rejoices in God my Savior. ...The mighty ones will be brought down from their thrones and the lowly lifted up." The message is clear—the birth of her child will bring the whole order of Rome and the world crashing down.

"The Kingdom"

Some of us might think that because we live in a democracy—a form of government in which the people wield the power—that the gospel poses no threat to our established order. We would be mistaken. None of the kingdoms of this world, including the United States of America, are the kingdom of God. They aren't even close. God's kingdom is radically different. The Greek word for kingdom is *basalia*, a realm ruled by a king or emperor. When we pray for this kingdom to come and then end by saying that the kingdom of this world belongs to God, we are acknowledging that if it belongs to God, it does not belong to Caesar. All the leaders of the world exercising power—even *we the people*—are mere pretenders to the throne. When Christians pray the Lord's Prayer, the White House, Congress, and the leaders of every nation should shake in their boots because what we are asking for is revolution.

The Lord's Prayer forces us to make a choice and decide where our allegiance lies. Will we be Americans first or citizens of heaven? God wants us to put our Christian ethics and concerns above those of our nation and personal interest. To say that the kingdom belongs to God is to say that this world belongs to God and one day God will have what God wants out of it.[63]

"The Power"

The next word, *power,* is *dynamos* in the Greek, and it is from this word that we get the word *dynamite*. It refers specifically to military power. To say that the power belongs to God is to trust in God's military strength. Just as we trust God to deliver us from temptation by the evil one, we trusting in God's power for our salvation. Our country might have the strongest military and largest nuclear arsenal, but we Christians believe that it is the Lord who has all the fire power. Psalm 20:7 says, "Some trust in chariots and some in horses," —the cutting-edge military weapons of the day—"but we trust in the name of the Lord our God." The leaders of the world might think they are in charge

---

63 See Chapter 6 Reflection Question 2.

and that military might can win the day, but it is the Lord who will prevail. Our security as Christians does not come from weaponry and war but from God. This part of the prayer has given great strength to Christians suffering from persecution or oppression. The jailor with his keys, the soldier with his guns, the slave master with his whip, and the politician with his legislation all have their power stripped from them and given to God.

"The Glory"

Finally, we get to the word glory or *doxa* in Greek, another political and military term that we have almost completely spiritualized. It means the honor and fame that come with a victory. Glory is what a king enjoys after a battle has been won. When we say that the glory belongs to God, we are saying that God alone is worthy to be praised for the victory. But we also recognize that God's victories look different from the glory of the world. John 12 reminds us that God is most glorified in the cross with the words, "I have glorified it and I will glorify it." God's glory is a peculiar glory. As the old hymn states, "in the cross of Christ that we glory.[64]" Christ the King reigns not from a throne but from a cross. This type of king comes to us riding on a donkey, and he wields his power by giving it away.

---

64 Fanny Crosby, "In the Cross of Christ I Glory"

Hope

This concluding doxology of the prayer, as a whole, is the Pledge of Allegiance for Christians. It is our proclamation that despite how things look, God is in charge, and God will reclaim God's kingdom, power, and glory. To pray this prayer is to call for a dramatic change in the social order. It is to swear allegiance to a coming kingdom.[65]

On Christmas Eve a few years ago, the New York Times ran an article about Edwin Shuman III, a Vietnam War hero, who passed away at eighty-two. He was a downed navy pilot who was held as a prisoner of war by the North Vietnamese in what was called the Hanoi Hilton. He was known for orchestrating a resistance in the POW camp of forty-three Americans. It was Christmastime, and he wanted to hold a church service and worship, but the atheist regime would not allow it. He decided to resist anyway and asked each member of the camp if they were committed to having church on Sunday. He asked person to person, because he knew that if they executed their plan it would lead to terrible punishment. A fellow prisoner, Leo K. Thorsness, recounted in a memoir — "He went around the cell pointing to each of us individually."

Mr. Thorsness continued. "When the 42nd man said yes, it was unanimous. At that instant, Ned knew he would end up in the torture cells."

The following Sunday, Commander Shuman stepped forward to lead worship, but the guards

---

65 See Chapter 6 Reflection Question 3.

quickly took him away. Then the next four ranking officers stepped forward, and they, too, were taken to the torture cells to be beaten. Meanwhile, as Mr. Thorsness told it, "the guards were now hitting P.O.W.s with gun butts and the cell was in chaos."

Then the sixth-ranking senior officer stepped forward to lead but this time he said, "Our Father" and the rest of the prisoners joined in to finish the prayer. The guards could not stop it this time, the prisoners were all praying in unison.

Mr. Thorsness, an Air Force pilot and recipient of the Medal of Honor, wrote in his memoir, *Surviving Hell: A POW's Journey* (2008):

> We won. They lost. Forty-two men in prison pajamas followed Ned's lead. I know I will never see a better example of pure raw leadership or ever pray with a better sense of the meaning of the words.[66]

When we pray the Lord's Prayer in church or in the home, it is easy to forget what these words mean. We are calling for a different social order and declaring that the world is not as it seems and that God is the King. N. T. Wright offers this perspective:

> If the church isn't prepared to subvert the kingdoms of this world with the kingdom of God, the only honest thing would be to give

---

[66] Edwin A. Shuman III, "Former Prisoner of War Who Defied Hanoi Hilton Guards, Dies at 82," By RICHARD GOLDSTEIN Published: December 24, 2013

up praying this prayer altogether, especially its final doxology.[67]

The ending of the Lord's Prayer is calling for a new order in the world.[68]

My friend, the Rev. Sean Peters, tells the story about going to a Chinese restaurant and at the end of his meal opening up his cookie to read his "fortune." It said, "Reality is reality." That is wisdom in our world. It is what it is. For Christians, there is a deeper truth. Peters states:

> Reality is reality! I get that, but I think that those of us who follow Jesus are actually called to something greater than hopeless pragmatism. The gospel message is primarily idealistic. It calls us to inaugurate the kingdom of God in the here and now—a kingdom where lions lay down with lambs; where every nation, tribe, people, and language stand before the throne of God in worship; where faith, hope, and love always trump fear, despair, and hatred. The biblical ideal of shalom demands that we refuse to see things as they are, but rather to see things as they should be. So, with all due respect to the little paper in my fortune cookie, I am choosing to believe that the kingdoms of this world will become the kingdoms of our God and of his Christ, and he shall reign forever and ever. And I'm choosing to believe that this idealistic king-

---

[67] N. T. Wright, *The Lord and His Prayer* (Grand Rapids: Eerdmans, 1996), pg. 67.

[68] See Chapter 6 Reflection Question 4.

dom can actually come, on earth as it is in heaven. It begins with me.[69]

Christians are people who believe that the world can change. Not only can it change; it will change. God's kingdom will come to earth.

Christians are not a cynical people; we are people of hope, but our hope is not in a political party or ideology or in electing the right candidate for president. Our hope is in Christ. Shane Claiborne and Chris Haw, in their book *Jesus for President: Politics for Ordinary Radicals*, draw a thought-provoking conclusion on this subject:

> The church has fallen in love with the state and this love affair is killing the church's imagination. Too often the patriotic values of pride and strength triumph over the spiritual virtues of humility gentleness and sacrificial love. Christian discipleship is politically and socially engaged, but in a way that confounds and transcends parties. It's easy to have political views—that's what politicians do. But it's much harder to embody a political alternative—that is what Saints do."

All of creation is waiting for the day that the church embodies a new politic, one shaped not by the sword or ballot box but by the cross. It is this

---

69   Sean Peters, Sermon FUMC Panama City, 2016.

politic that is the hope of the world. There is nothing more political than the love of God and the love of neighbor.

When we say that the kingdom, power, and glory is God's forever and ever, we are talking about the second coming of Christ. Christians are an eschatological people, a future-focused people. When we say the creeds, the last third is about what we believe is coming. Christians believe that the future of the world is the kingdom of God. Christians, therefore, are a hopeful people with big dreams.[70] We can say with St. Julian of Norwich, "All shall be well."

I once had an outside consultant visit to give me some ideas about my church and community and how it could grow and prosper. He said that the one thing that held our community back was the lack of a hopeful imagination. It can be hard to imagine the world as different from what it is, but that is what praying for the kingdom does. It causes us to develop a holy discontent and begin to imagine a different world. I believe what holds us back is that we want to base our future on the past when God has a dream that is new.

Richard Lischer tells a story about a nursing home that he visited where many of the patients used to be well-known scholars. Today they suffer terribly from illnesses that have reduced many of them to just staring out the window. But on these residents' doors are photographs from their young-

---

70   See Chapter 6 Reflection Question 5.

er days when they were in their prime. He goes on to state:

> So on the outside of the door, the visitor sees an attractive, commanding presence; inside, in the room, the future. The photos are the nursing home's way of saying: Have a little respect. This is who she used to be. She was once beautiful and accomplished; he was once handsome and powerful. Have a little respect. It's a lovely gesture but slightly off-target in that it implies we should love people because of what they once were. I think that when the thief on the cross said to Jesus, "Remember me," he wasn't saying, "Remember what a nice guy I used to be." I think he was saying, "Take me as I am. Receive me." And when Jesus forgave the thief on the cross, I don't think he saw a clean-cut kid who had made a few bad decisions and squandered his potential. I think he saw a thief—on a cross. And he dreamed him into paradise.[71]

In this part of the Lord's Prayer, Jesus dreams us into paradise. God has a dream for the world. It is saints who see it and begin to live it. Martin Luther King, Jr. caught a glimpse of the dream and lived in such a way to make it a reality. God is dreaming us into paradise. This dream is not based on who we are. It is not based on our past. The title of Lischer's sermon says it all, "Your Dreams Are Too Small."

---

71 Richard Lischer, "Your Dreams Are Too Small," Sermon Duke Chapel 2016.

Realizing that the kingdom, power, and glory belong to God calls us to see a new reality. The kingdom, power, and glory already belong to God, but the world does not yet know it. In order to reveal the kingdom, we must dream God-sized dreams and hope and pray for a better future. The bad news we see on TV is not reality. It does not have to be this way. The Lord's Prayer teaches us that there is a coming reality that is already here in part—the kingdom, power, and glory of God.[72]

Reflection Questions

1. In what ways does this final phrase summarize the whole prayer?
2. Why should Christians praying the Lord's Prayer make the powers that be "shake in their boots?"
3. Why does the prayer use such politically charged terms like kingdom, power, and glory?
4. What does it mean to say the Lord's Prayer is subversive of the natural order?
5. Why are Christians a hopeful people? Where does our hope lie?
6. What kind of dreams does God have for your life, family, church, and community?

---

72 See Chapter 6 Reflection Question 6.

7

Amen

A certain man bought a donkey from a preacher. This donkey had been trained in a unique way, and the preacher explained the commands to the donkey's new owner. The only way to make the donkey go was to exclaim, "Hallelujah!"

The only way to make the donkey stop was to say, "Amen!" This was a Christian donkey! The new owner was pleased with his new donkey and immediately took it for a ride to try out the commands. "Hallelujah!" shouted the man, and the donkey began to trot. "Amen!" shouted the man, and the donkey stopped immediately. He was very pleased, and with another "Hallelujah," he rode off toward home.

The man traveled through some mountains and inadvertently came upon a cliff. Suddenly he could not remember the commands.

"Stop," yelled the man. "Halt!" Yet the donkey kept going. Remembering that the commands were churchy words, he yelled out, "Bible! Jesus! Mary! Joseph! Jehoshaphat!" And then in desperation, the man just offered a prayer, "Dear Lord, please make this donkey stop! In Jesus' name, Amen." The donkey came to an abrupt stop just one step from the edge of the cliff. The man was so thrilled with gratitude that he shouted a resounding, "Hallelujah!"[73]

---

[73] This joke does not originate with me but has been handed down by many preachers.

Endings are important. I have learned that the old saying, "All is well that ends well" is true. No matter how terrible things get, if a happy ending is possible, it makes everything better. This is why Christians have hope. We believe that the world will end well. We call this doctrine the *parousia*, meaning "the coming" or "the presence." One day Christ's presence will fully saturate the cosmos. There will be a new heaven and new earth, and Christ will fill all and all. Endings, therefore, are important.

At the end of the Lord's Prayer, it seems as though we have said everything that needs to be said. But one more word—*Amen*—must be uttered. Although it's one believers use frequently, it might be the most overlooked word in all of Christianity because we fail to realize how unusual it is to pray with such a word. There are only two Hebrew words that were part of ancient Israelite worship that have been preserved through the ages. They were incorporated in to the ancient Greek liturgy of the early church, maintained when Rome transformed the mass into Latin, and continue to be left untranslated in almost every language as the Reformation insisted that Christian services be done in the vernacular. Those words are *hallelujah*, which means praise the Lord, and then the most common, *amen*, which is used in Judaism, Christianity, and Islam. It might be the most commonly used word in the world.[74]

---

74 See Chapter 7 Reflection Question 1.

Not Just a Final Word

It is strange that the meaning of what may be the most commonly used word is unknown to most of the world. For most of us, amen is not a word as much as it is punctuation—think period or exclamation point. It does, however, have a meaning. It is rooted in the Hebrew word for belief or faith, and when it is translated, which is rarely, it is translated as, "so be it,", "truly," or "verily." It occurs three different ways in scripture. The one we are most familiar with is the *final amen*, which concludes a thought or a prayer. It also can occur completely separate from other comments, affirming the thought of another as in the *detached amen*. The third amen is the way that Jesus seemed to have it used most. He did not, as far as we know, end prayers with amen, but what we have clear evidence of is that he began sermons or his most important sayings, with the *initial amen*.

Unfortunately, the initial amen is difficult to see because translators have attempted to give us a paraphrase of what they think it means. Every time that Jesus says, "Truly, truly, I say unto you" or "Verily, verily," he is using the word *amen*. These amen statements are so common in scripture that Jesus reminds me of the savant character Raymond from the 1988 film "Rain Man," who in his brilliance repeats certain words over and over again. Jesus seems stuck on this word; it is his favorite. Whenever he says "amen" or "Truly," it is a clue that he is about to say something very important. It is a hint that he is about to zero in on his target and proclaim the most basic truth.

What Is Truth?

Saying "amen" is to say that something is true. In a world in which everything is relative, how do we find truth? This question is as old as Pontius Pilot as he asked Jesus, "What is truth?" Jesus' answer is telling. He just stood there, as if to say, "I am right here." In John's Gospel, Jesus says, "I am the way, the truth, and the life." Jesus is there proclaimed as the embodiment of truth. What if truth is not a logical position or an argument but a person? Another way to think about ultimate truth is reality. What if Jesus is the ultimate reality and the things that we most often mistake for reality are not real at all? This is what the Book of Revelation proclaims when it gives a strange and special title to Jesus. In Revelation 3:14, Jesus is called "The Amen." When reality is revealed, which is the apocalypse, a revealing, and we see the world as it really is, we will see Christ. It is the Great Amen who gives us the power and ability to say, "Amen."[75]

Some churches have what is called the "amen corner." This is a group of people who are paying attention to the service and sermon, and when they hear a point that they know is true, they call out "Amen." This ministry of affirmation is important. In many traditions, it means "give us more of this," and the preacher knows to emphasize that point

---

75   See Chapter 7 Reflection Question 2.

even more. To be a part of the "amen corner" is to have a ministry of affirmation and to highlight the kingdom of God wherever we see it. To learn to pray "amen" fully is to learn to say yes to God wherever God is working. It is to offer encouragement to those doing the work of Christ in the world by helping those in need and serving the poor. It is to affirm the kingdom of heaven wherever we find it. The Lord's Prayer calls us to join God's "amen corner" of the world and herald the coming kingdom.[76]

Faith in a God Who Listens

The most basic meaning of *amen* is to offer words of faith that our prayers will be answered. Jesus taught us to pray to a God who answers prayer. Theologically, we begin with the "amen" in mind. Karl Barth says that, "we must begin with the end, that is, we must first consider the answer to prayer."[77] As Christians, we begin with the fact that God indeed answers prayers. If we did not believe this, there would be no reason to pray. We can fall into the modern habit of believing that prayer is self-therapy, but prayer is about a God who listens and answers.

The Heidelberg Catechism teaches us that "the answer to our prayer is more certain than our awareness of the thing that we request."[78] It is remarkable to think that God's answer to our prayer

---

76 See Chapter 7 Reflection Question 3.
77 Karl Barth, *Prayer*, 50th Anniversary ed. (Louisville: Westminster John Knox Press, 2022), 13.
78 Heidelberg Catechism, Question 129.

is more certain than even our prayer itself. This is a theological reminder that prayer is not based on our techniques or skills or our limited theological vocabulary. It is based on God, who came to us as Jesus Christ and continues to listen to us. Or as Barth says, "Our prayers are weak and poor. Nevertheless, what matters is not that our prayers be forceful, but that God listens to them. That is why we pray."

Many people wonder if God indeed answers prayer. As Christians, we must say, "Yes!" We are more certain of God and God's answer than we are of ourselves and our questions! To believe that God answers prayers does not mean that we will get everything that we want. When God answers prayers, we do not necessarily get what we want. We get what God wants. One of the chief objectives of the Lord's Prayer is to teach us to want what God wants—primarily for God's kingdom to come and for God's will to be done. But isn't it wonderful that God also wants us to have daily bread, to be forgiven, and to be delivered from evil in a world that is marked by a lack of truth, and where everything is relative? It is the Lord's Prayer that teaches Christians what truth is. We are confident and certain of God's work in the world. We are more confident of this than we are of ourselves.[79]

Martin Luther taught that the Amen was one of the most important parts of prayer. He said that when we say it, we should "speak it firmly." All too

---

[79] See Chapter 7 Reflection Question 4

often our prayers are followed by weak *amens* instead of an exclamation of confidence. Luther also said:

> Never doubt that God in his mercy will surely hear you and say "yes" to your prayers. Never think that you are kneeling or standing alone, rather think that the whole of Christendom, all devout Christians, are standing there beside you and you are standing among them in a common, united petition which God cannot disdain. Do not leave your prayer without having said or thought, "Very well. God has heard my prayer; this I know as a certainty and a truth." That is what Amen means.[80]

When we offer the final amen, we join the "amen corner" with a mighty chorus of saints and with the confidence that God indeed answers prayers. God—Father, Son, and Holy Spirit—loves us and cares for us and longs to listen to and answer our prayers.

Held Together

I spent part of my chaplaincy education at a large psychiatric hospital. What I dreaded most was having to preach and lead a chapel service. The patients who were institutionalized in this hospital were quite ill. In the Alzheimer's wing, there were

---

80 Martin Luther, "A Practical Way to Pray" (1535), in *Martin Luther's Basic Theological Writings*, 2d ed., ed. Timothy Lull (Minneapolis: Fortress Press, 2012), 35.

dozens of patients who could not remember the names of their loved ones or even their own names. The rest of the hospital was filled with people suffering from terrible mental illness, such as schizophrenia and dissociative disorders.

I had never seen a place like that before. It was my job, once a week, to lead the patients in worship. For the most part, they were unresponsive. I felt as though I were completely wasting my time. (It's hard enough to know if psychologically healthy people are listening to a sermon or paying attention during worship—not that I have ever preached to a group that was normal!) Leading worship at that hospital, I always felt as if I were a complete failure. It was like preaching to a brick wall—at least until the end of the service. Each week I would lead them in a prayer that would conclude, "Now as our Savior Christ hath taught us, we are bold to pray." Then all of a sudden people throughout the room, who were facing challenges that most us will never have to face began to pray along. "Our Father, who art in heaven …" I would see Alzheimer's patients who could not remember the names of their children whisper every word of the prayer like a secret.

Many would have tears running down their faces because in that moment things came together for them. Other patients who seemed completely disconnected from what we call reality, lost in a world of their own, would join the community in prayer. When we reached the "Amen," things got exciting. Everybody, no matter their ability, could pray that word. Some yelled it out, and then everybody would laugh and laugh. It was everyone's favorite part of the service, not the music or the preaching, but the Lord's Prayer and its great amen. It was as if we each knew who we were or maybe better yet, we knew who God was, and in light of that fact, who we were made less of a difference. For me, it was proof that the efficacy of our prayers is not based on our efforts and ability but on God's.

When we pray the word *amen,* we can be comforted that prayer is not about us, who we are, or what we have done. It is about a God who listens, a God who holds us together when we can't hold ourselves, a God who knows us when we don't know ourselves. We join in saying the same word used by the matriarchs and patriarchs of Israel, the same word Jesus constantly uttered, the most used word of the early church's mothers and fathers, a word uttered by sinners and saints throughout history and around the world.

We are asking God to make it happen. We don't quite know what the "it" will be, but when "it" arrives, the world will be healed, we will know who we really are, and God's reality will be revealed. To pray *amen* is to rest in a certainty that our lives and this whole world belongs to a God that Jesus taught us to call "Our Father." It is the amen that holds the prayer together—just as Jesus Christ, the Great Amen, holds all things together (Colossians 1:17) and brings them to their full and final conclusion. [81]

---

81 See Chapter 7 Reflection Question 5.

Reflection Questions

1. What does the word "amen" mean to you?
2. Why do you think that the Book of Revelation calls Jesus "the Amen"?
3. What could you do to be more a part of God's "Amen corner?" What is going on in the world in which you can say "Amen?"
4. Do you believe God answers prayers? Has God ever answered your prayer but with the opposite answer you were expecting?
5. How does the *amen* hold the prayer together? How does God hold us together as our Great Amen, when we can no longer hold our lives together?

Scripture Index

Leviticus 20:26 12

Psalm 37:4 19

Matthew 6 20
Matthew 6:8 21
Matthew 7:12 51
Matthew 18 51
Matthew 18:22 57

Luke 4 48
Luke 5:20 7
Luke 12 34
Luke 22 72

Romans 12 15
Romans 8 9, 21
Romans 8:34 7

1 Corinthians 3 14

2 Corinthians 11:14 69
Hebrews 7:25 7
Hebrews 12 7

James 1:17 40
James 4:7 70

1 Peter 1:16 12
1 Peter5:8 72

1 John 2:1 7

Revelation 3:14 92